Blur

Jon Ewing

This edition published 1996 by
Parragon Book Service Ltd
Unit 13-17 Avonbridge Trading Estate,
Atlantic Rd, Avonmouth, Bristol BS11 9QD
by Carlton Books
20 St. Anne's Court
London W1V 3AW

ISBN 0.75251.858.5

Printed and bound in Italy

Acknowledgments
The publisher would like to thank the following sources for their kind
permission to reproduce the pictures in this book.

All Action/Sue Moore, Nick Tansley; London Features/Piers Allardyce, Matt
Anker, Andrew Catlin, Jeff Davy, David Fisher, Colin Mason, Ilpo Musto,
Andy Phillips, Derek Ridgers; Pictorial Press/Rob Verhorst; Retna/Matt
Anker, Kelly Ashmore, Colin Bell, Adrian Boot, Jeffy Davy, Steve Double,
Karl Grant, Adrian Green, Alastair Indge, Michael Putland, Steve Pyke,
Paul Rider, Ed Sirrs, Paul Slattery, Steve Speller; Rex Features/Dave Hogan,
Ilpo Musto, Brian Rasic, Richard Young; S.I.N/ Piers Allardyce, Peter
Anderson, Melanie Cox, Steve Double, Martyn Goodacre, Liane Hentscher,
Hayley Madden, Doralba Picerno, Roy Tee, Kim Tonelli, Andy Willsher.

Every effort has been made to acknowledge correctly and contact the
source and/or copyright holder of each picture, and Carlton Books
Limited apologises for any unintentional errors or omissions which
will be corrected in future editions of this book

Contents

Baggy Trousers

A lot of bands like to tell you that they don't care about fame and money. As long as they can make music, they say, it doesn't matter about getting to the top of the charts; and if other people like what they're doing, that's a bonus. But Blur were never that way. They had a goal from the very beginning: to smash the bandwagons that stood in their way — baggy bands, shoegazers, grunge rockers — and stand head and shoulders above them all as the most popular music-makers in Britain. And maybe, eventually, the world...

Damon Albarn was lucky — he could very well have been called Dweezil or Moon Unit. There's no escaping the fact that his mum and dad were a couple of idealistic, pot-smoking, summer-of-loving hippies.

The Albarn family has its roots Lincolnshire. Damon's father, Keith, came from a family of Quakers, and his mother was from farming stock, but they gave up the rural lifestyle to be artists, and ran away to London in the Sixties. Damon's

Damon Albarn (born: March 23, 1968)

mum became a stage designer for Joan Littlewood's highly respected theatre company. When Damon came along on March 23, 1968, Keith Albarn was running an ambitious company devising 'environmental happenings' — the hippie version of a multimedia installation that combined art, theatre, music or whatever came to hand to challenge artistic conventions. He was also involved in pioneering arts programming on British TV, studying Islamic design, managing influential art rock band Soft Machine and putting on an exhibition by Yoko Ono. Together, they all lived in a small, terraced house in Leytonstone, East London, where the Albarns entertained famous names from the rock world in a smoke-filled room with silver-painted walls lined with books.

Damon went to George Thompson primary school in the East End of London until the age of ten, when Keith was offered a job as an art lecturer. While his parents organized the move, Damon went with some friends of the family on a trip to Turkey, but when he came back from this trip of a lifetime, his new home was a major anticlimax. Colchester, a sleepy, rural town near the south-east coast of England, had none of the excitement and colour of London, let alone

Turkey. Damon felt out of place in Stanway Comprehensive school and his personality abruptly changed. 'That's where I became the violin-playing extrovert,' Damon says now. 'I turned from being an urban child into a complete country child and went fishing and watched birds and things like that. I couldn't fit in at all with the lads then. I was the weirdo. Posh-stroke-gay. I always got called gay. "Oy, poof! Gayboy!" '

Damon was a loner, if not by choice then simply because nobody really liked him. He had a cocky attitude at school. His opening remark to Graham Coxon — 'Those aren't proper brogues,' he said, pointing to the young lad's shoes — might easily have led to a fight, but instead developed into a symbiotic friendship which has lasted for the rest of their lives. Not surprisingly, Graham didn't like him much to begin with. 'I thought he was a vain wanker,' he recalls, but somehow he must have seen something of himself in the maverick musician and after a while Graham 'realized he was actually quite a generous and caring geezer'.

Graham had come to Colchester from Derby a couple of years before Damon, although he was born in Berlin on

March 12, 1969 where his father was stationed in the army as a clarinet and saxophone player in the Worcestershire & Sherwood Foresters regiment. Not surprisingly, music was introduced to him at a very early age — apparently, the first instrument he ever played was a fife (a small flute used in military bands), and he was playing drums and sax while his age was still in single figures. He got his first guitar aged twelve and was hooked immediately.

His dad, who left the army to conduct the Essex Police Band, tried brainwashing him with jazz but,

Graham Coxon (born: March 12, 1969)

fortunately for the world, Graham resisted. He started off by playing along to records — the first song he mastered on the guitar was 'Aunties & Uncles', a Jam B-side. He was a devoted music fan, spending all of his money on records and music magazines.

Damon, on the other hand, knew very little about the music scene of the early Eighties. His parents had let him express himself to the extent that he had a Jam logo painted on the wall of their garage, but he wasn't a devoted music fan like most other kids. His house was very much the home of artists and thinkers. 'Round his house I wouldn't see any records,' says Graham. 'There'd be a stuffed fox and trays full of fossils, and books.

'I'd play him records I thought were incredible and he'd absorb them,' Graham continues. 'So I *programmed* him.'

Life as a London tart

The two lads quickly became an inseparable and incorrigible duo. 'Graham and I went through the Funny Time together,' says Damon. 'You know, school, adolescence... even if he always disappeared when I got into fights.'

The first time they got drunk together was on elderflower wine made by Damon's dad. They cooled it in

Dave Rowntree (born: May 8, 1964)

"The best thing about being in a band is that you can allow your insanities to develop.

And get paid for it."

Alex

Alex James (born: November 1, 1968)

the river and sat under a tree getting their first taste of adult freedom... It all sounds like a delightful rites-of-passage story. 'Just like Enid Blyton,' says Graham; until you hear the sordid outcome. 'We got so wrecked that I crapped on my jumper!' he confesses. 'I wanted a poo and I forgot it was tied round my waist. I had to throw it into someone's garden!'

After he had met Graham, Damon started to write songs. His first was about a diamond run from Amsterdam to Johannesburg — even then, as now, his inspiration was a

Arguably the most successful band of the 'shoegazing' era, Oxford art school four-piece Ride dominated the indie scene in 1991 while baggy rivals the Stone Roses were lost in legal limbo.

programme on TV. And even then he had the famous arrogance which inspired him to become famous, just to prove everyone else was wrong. That aimless, big ambition finally took shape when one night he was watching Morrissey on *The South Bank Show*. 'You know what made me want to be in a band?' asks Damon. 'It was... hearing Morrissey say that pop music was dead, and that The Smiths had been the last group of any importance. I was round at Graham's house... And I remember thinking, No one is going to tell me that pop music is finished.'

Their first 'jam sessions' were playing Sixties' cover versions at school. 'Graham and I used to spend every lunchtime and every first break in the music hut,' Damon remembers vividly. 'We'd play the piano and saxophone and guitar and do covers of loads of Sixties' songs, folk songs,

musical songs, anything. We had no choice, as a lot of school songbooks of that period were Simon & Garfunkel, Lennon & McCartney — that's what we were given.'

However, although Graham and Damon played music together, their first band was a long way off. Graham's favoured instrument was still the sax and he reached a grade five at school, while Damon took A-level Music and

failed. After the Sixth Form they parted ways. Damon couldn't wait to get out of the town. ('They hate us in Colchester now,' he admits. 'Well, they hate me in particular. They won't even play our records in the record shops there.') He got a place at a London drama college called East 15, while Graham stayed in Essex to take a two-year diploma course in General Art & Design while working part-time in a Sainsbury's supermarket, the strain of which, reveals Damon, made him ill and hospitalized him.

Damon's drama career was no more successful. He was assigned theatrical exercises and improvizations, like dressing in women's clothing and travelling on the London Underground acting like a tart. Being a natural extrovert, he wasn't especially embarrassed, but he didn't feel he was learning much from the experience, either. After a year he decided that it was a waste of time — or, in his words, 'It was so up its own arse'.

A drop in the acid pool

One good thing did come out of his studies, however — he worked with the Berliner Ensemble, at a festival in Harlow dedicated to the work of Berthold Brecht (or, more

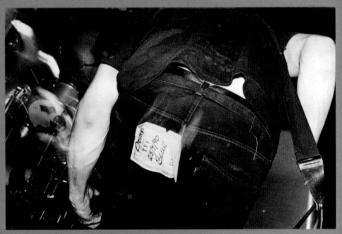

Damon: 'We were in very deep water in our early days because, basically, we didn't know what we were doing... We were a fledgling group having a laugh.'

Damon: 'We're early Eighties nuclear children, a product of our times, and our time is now.'

Damon writes most of Blur's songs but the publishing royalties are split between the band in a hierarchy of contributors: Damon gets almost half, Graham a little over a quarter, Alex about half that much and Dave about one-eighth.

accurately, to Kurt Weill, the composer who wrote the music for Brecht's plays and lyrics). From this experience he acquired his love of Teutonic waltzes which would give such a distinctive colour to Blur's songs. Damon's later girlfriend, Justine Frischmann, wouldn't always agree. 'Justine hates my waltzes,' he says, 'because she says they remind her of Hitler and the Nazis. I like the dreadfulness of it all.'

Through all this, he continued to write songs and play his own music, and formed an ill-fated duo called Two's A Crowd, with a character named Sam — an act which reputedly combined the use of physical theatre and synthesizers. The mind boggles.

For his nineteenth birthday, Damon's granddad gave him £3,000 to go into a recording studio called The Beat Factory. The resulting demos would be worth a small fortune now, but Damon has no intention of allowing them to be heard, swearing that they are 'utterly vacuous' and 'hopelessly unfocused'. After the session, the studio boss offered him a job as a general dogsbody. He didn't get paid, but Damon was allowed to have a set of keys and free recording time when the studio wasn't busy.

Around this time, he dropped out and went on the dole for a while. 'When I was about twenty I went through a period of getting locked up because I used to get drunk. That's when I started to mutate slowly into what I am today... whatever I am.'

He did a few odd jobs to pay the rent, making coffee at Le Croissant on Euston Station and tending bar at the flash Portobello Hotel, where he met Bono and the Edge, among other rock stars. Meanwhile, after years as a loner he started to come out of his shell and get in with a new crowd of friends. 'I started taking drugs then,' says Damon. 'I did my first acid in a crappy little flat in Lewisham. I started to become less of an outsider to the world, slowly sort of returning to earth in a weird way. That's the strange thing — it made me come closer to reality. It was taking away the uptightness I had about not wanting to be like anybody else on any level... I thought I was important. I was one of those people that really had to become quite successful to feel normal.'

Hot water bottle player

His next stab at fame was on the stage of Colchester Arts Centre in 1988, a 'very theatrical' one-man show playing to about fifteen people who didn't exactly bring the house down. However, that night his false start of a career finally got a push when he met Graham who was with a new friend, Dave Rowntree.

Dave was a few years older than the two school friends. Compared to the boyish good looks of Graham and Damon, his face was sharp, his skin drained and unpigmented — pretty scary-looking until you looked

closer, into his clear, cherubic, blue eyes. He was born (May 8, 1964) and bred in Colchester but had already seen a bit of the world — he'd spent some time living in London and in France, playing in a band before crawling back to Colchester to become a computer programmer.

Like Damon and Graham, Dave had musical roots. His mum was a pianist in an orchestra, his father was a sound engineer for the BBC and commuted to and from London every day for forty years. Dave started out playing a chanter (an instrument similar to the bagpipes; like 'playing a hot water bottle,' Dave explains, disdainfully) and then graduated to drums. He didn't study music and he wasn't much of an academic, but he had a flair for maths and an interest, which remains today, in computers, so he went to Woolwich to do a Higher National Diploma in computer science.

Having received his diploma he still felt unready for a career, and instead formed a three-piece 'jazz punk' band — called Idle Vice. This was while he was living in a squat in north London's Crouch End for six months before going — for no particular reason — to tour around France, busking and playing in seedy clubs for two years.

After that, Idle Vice just fizzled out and Dave came home. He had a mohawk haircut, but he still looked respectable enough to get a job with the local council as a programmer. He met Graham in a pub in Colchester, which in turn led to his being at Damon's one-man show, from which he left with the parting words: 'If you ever need a drummer, give me a ring.' Of course, that call came soon after. 'I had an executive, sitting-behind-a-desk, high-powered job,' says Dave. 'And I gave that up to be a drummer!'

Briefly they formed a band, calling themselves Circus and playing a few local gigs in a line-up which featured Damon, Graham, Damon's friend Eddy and sometimes Dave. However, there wasn't much of a future in it and Graham

Alex: 'We're just boozers, really. It's as bad as anything else, but you get spared the claptrap. It's a good pop drug.'

wasn't quite ready to give up his career to be in a band. Instead he chose the academic path and went to New Cross in south-east London to study fine arts at Goldsmith's College. There he met bassist Alex James and the future line-up of Blur was united.

'We pretty soon discovered that we had a lot in common,' says Alex.

'Booze and guitars,' clarifies Graham.

Feeble Seymour gets the mace

Alex (born November 1, 1968) was from sleepy, southern, seaside Bournemouth, and enjoyed an unmusical family background — his father was a retired forklift truck salesman. Alex bought himself a Fender guitar for his

Alex: 'I quite like the idea of being a renaissance humanist. Not just interested in music but in science and art. Because being in a pop band is like being an empathy sink.'

sixteenth birthday, although admits that at his school everyone had a guitar 'as a fashion accessory, like you do'.

'To be cool in the first year you had to be good at football,' he continues, 'In the third year you had to have a girlfriend and in the fifth year you had to be in a band. That was that.'

Alex didn't exactly live an exciting life. He once made a recording of 'The Chain' by Fleetwood Mac and tried to pass it off as his own band to his (presumably sadly gullible) mates. He excelled at school — although he had virtually no training in music. 'My music teacher has been sent to prison for being a buttock fondler, which may explain why I never took music lessons,' he points out. Before going to Goldsmith's, where he would meet Graham, he took a year off, during which he worked on building sites and in a Safeway supermarket, on the cheese counter. His early claims to fame were: 'I helped to rebuild a nuclear power station once,' and 'I dropped acid before I went to work for the first time. And I had to work there for another six months.'

Topping the UK album chart with
Doubt in 1991, Jesus Jones were by
far Food's biggest hitmakers until
Blur's big break in 1994.

In his year off he did manage to form his first band
— Mr Pang's Bang Bangs, named in honour of his
landlord. Like most people, when Alex first met Graham's
mate, Damon, he wasn't impressed. 'He completely pissed
me off,' Alex recalls. However, in time Alex learned to see
through Damon's sour layer of defences and before long
they began to play music together, Damon on keyboards
and vocals, Graham on guitar, Alex on bass and Dave on
drums. It's hard to say when they started to get serious.
Their early gigs were just a bit of a laugh. Early
impromptu performances included a party at Goldsmith's,
and a railway museum in a village somewhere outside
Colchester. When their first gig proper came along, they
had to think of a name, and they came up with the feeble
idea of Seymour.

Seymour is the name of a character in a story by *The
Catcher In The Rye* author, JD Salinger, who marries, goes on
honeymoon and then blows his brains out. Seymour made
their official debut at Dingwall's in Camden Lock — now home
to the Jongleurs cabaret club — supporting forgotten
luminaries New Fast Automatic Daffodils and Too Much Texas.
Their first ever review, in the trade magazine *Music Week*,
credited them as Feymour. Sadly, the gig ended with a trip to
the hospital thanks to the antics of their mate, Adam, who
whipped out his tackle in public. The bouncers were not
amused and promptly sprayed the entire band with Mace, the
chemical aerosol designed for the self-defence of rape victims.

Pyjama trousers and sad anoraks

Still, you've got to start somewhere. During 1989, Seymour
played a few gigs — no one seems quite sure how many,
including the band — at poky little London venues like The

Cricketers, Kennington and The Pied Bull, Islington, and — thanks to Damon's studio connection — they recorded a demo featuring a track called 'She's So High'. They weren't much good back then, but they were having fun and slowly learning the fine art of working an audience. 'It's great being in a band when you're that age,' says Damon, 'thinking about what you want to be, doing manifestos, thinking about your image, all that... We did a couple of gigs and people were really talking about us and we got signed almost straight away. We were really arrogant, but that's part of this job — you need arrogance, self-confidence.'

That arrogance has been prevalent in most of Damon's interviews ever since. Comments like 'I've always known I'm incredibly special', are commonplace in Blur's cuttings. 'It's not a big deal,' Damon will say. 'We've always wanted to be stars.'

The truth is perhaps a little more mundane. Like millions of bands before them, they spent months locked in a rehearsal and 'worked and worked on making ourselves brilliant', in Damon's words. They all started out with talent, but it would take a while to turn that into a distinctive — and commercial — sound of their own. Damon and Graham, of course, both had formal training in music, as did Dave, who is literate in percussion notation. Alex, although he gave up music lessons early on, can still read music, which makes the band's rehearsals a lot simpler, as Damon explains: 'If we say in jams "Eight bars of E, two bars of C, *del capo*", we all know what it means.'

They touted their tape from one record company to another without success until one day 'She's So High' landed on the desk of Andy Ross of Food Records. Ross, an economics graduate and former music journalist for *Sounds* magazine, went to see the band immediately and was mildly disappointed. As he remembers it, Dave was wearing pyjama

Damon's necklace: 'My mum made it for me years ago and it's part of me now. It was meant to protect me when she wasn't there. I think it's worked, on the whole.'

"The only tradition I've ever felt comfortable with is the British art-school group tradition and when I think about some of the groups from that background I'd probably rather be like the Talking Heads."

Damon

"The first time I stayed at Damon's, he took me for a **drive** and **crashed,** and then told me he didn't have a **driving licence** — so I had to tell his mum I did it."

Alex

Damon on influences: 'I think we're a very Nineties band - the only Nineties band around. If you're gonna analyse a set of individuals and their music, you've got to look further than what you see on the record. Journalists always try to look further without knowing enough.'

trousers and the band were, in his words 'shambolic' and 'sartorially challenged'. Most people who were there seem to agree. 'They were wearing stripy tops,' says journalist Holly Martens, 'and sounding like the kitchen sink falling down a flight of stairs.' However, history proves that Food signed them up anyway with a not-so-princely advance of £3,000.

Unfortunately, Andy Ross was only one half of Food Records. The label was started in 1984 by David Balfe, former manager of the Teardrop Explodes, and the relationship between Balfe and his new signings was delicate from the very beginning. For a start, he was the

one who insisted on scrapping the name Seymour. 'Balfe said it sounded like a sad anorak band,' says Graham. 'Which we fucking well were!'

Blurred and baggy

The band were given a list of possible names, which happened to include Blur, as well as The Shining Path and Sub. (Incidentally, among their other choices were Sensitize and Whirlpool, names later picked up by other bands in the Food stable but now long forgotten.) 'This has probably passed into legend as record company manipulation,' Ross

Live in Rotterdam, August 1991.

says, without a hint of repentance. 'But you either give a band carte blanche or else you kick 'em up the arse and take out the crap bits.'

Looking back, they admit that their bosses were probably right. Damon, typically, has a philosophical reason for it. 'Seymour was our obtuse side,' he muses. 'It's like if you're schizophrenic and spend six months in an institution; they cure you by leading you to the conclusion that you're better off with one side of your personality than skipping between two. I didn't think we'd do well with our obtuse side, so we made less of it. Half our personality is latent, like the sort of relationship where the physical side works best if you both dress up in leather.' Hmm...

Early in 1990, under pressure from their new masters, Damon, Graham, Dave and Alex signed on the dotted line and agreed to be known as Blur. Then the publicity mill started to churn. Thanks to Ross, before they even had a record out, Blur had appeared on the front cover of *Sounds*, and they were being prematurely squeezed into that over-crowded pigeonhole marked Next Big Thing.

But the rest of the world wasn't quite ready for them. In October 1990, 'She's So High' was released to an indifferent public that promptly dismissed the record as a second-rate stowaway on the 'baggy' bandwagon. In fairness, that wasn't far from the truth. The eponymously titled debut album by Manchester's Stone Roses in 1989 had set in motion a major new wave of British music which combined the heavy grooves of acid house music with the pop sensibilities of indie guitar bands. The baggy label came from the accompanying fashion attire — loose-fitting jeans, oversized T-shirts and hooded, tie-dyed tops, usually

Damon: 'I don't really head-bang, I just lurch about banging myself on the head with my microphone. But the mike is in my hand, so it's not as bad as it looks. Tricks of the trade!'

Tim Smith of the indefinable Cardiacs, a great influence on Damon's songwriting. Check out their LP *A Little Man And A House And The Whole World Window* for a taster.

listenable, simplistic dance pop, heavily over-produced by Steve Lovell and Steve Power, with so much reverberation on the chorus that the lyrics can barely be understood.

Perhaps its only legacy was the memorable, and teasingly controversial, sleeve art featuring a naked woman riding a giant pig. It was the first Blur artwork to be designed by Stylorouge, the company which would gradually develop the band's distinctive image as their career went on, from snippets of Fifties, advertising to airbrushed Seventies, poster art to the credit card mock-ups which promoted the singles on *The Great Escape*.

Top of the teenybops

1991 would turn out to be a big success, a year in which Damon would begin to achieve the fame he had always dreamed of. The turning point was in April, with the release of the band's second single, 'There's No Other Way'. Although once again a product of baggy pop culture, it was distinctive and hummable enough to rate among the most popular of its generation, along with the Stone Roses' 'Fools Gold', 'I'm Free' by the Soup Dragons and 'Groovy Train' by the Farm.

'There's No Other Way' seems to belong to another more nostalgic era — the softened Hammond keyboards and sitar-effect guitars reek of Sixties commercial psychedelic pop that wouldn't sound out-of-place on *The Best of The Monkees*. It's the recipe for perfect pop — a highly contagious chorus, a liquid guitar riff and words that are easy, almost irresistible to sing along to. Okay, so the baggy drum beat is generic and derivative, but it works, and Damon's lyrics, obsessed with 'watching' from the sidelines while the world goes by, are as typical of his writing style as any he's ever written. And it's all wrapped up in less than three-and-a-half minutes, leaving you panting for more. As Blur's first major British tour got

accompanied by a pudding basin hair cut with a fringe hanging down over the eyes. Baggy fashion spread like wildfire across the country and the sound seized the imagination of both press and public alike. Bands like Flowered Up, Northside, the Soup Dragons and the Farm all found some degree of chart success on the baggy bandwagon, but like the Roses themselves, their days were numbered. As the scene ran its course, the indie scene began to incorporate more imaginative interpretations of dance culture and baggy soon became redundant.

Meanwhile, 'She's So High' was yet another simple-minded and contrived addition to a long list of tedious and generic records, an inauspicious arrival on the music scene which did Blur very few favours.

It begins with a gentle sweep of guitar breaking into a solo laconic rock'n'roll riff which, in retrospect, isn't a million miles from the Oasis hit 'Roll With It' — it's Graham and Damon struggling to weigh up commercial appeal against their own aimless musical aspirations. As such, it is under way, 'There's No Other Way' surprised everyone — not least the band and their record label — by entering the charts at No. 20. After a performance on *Top Of The Pops* and the support of the nation's radio stations, it rapidly climbed up the charts until, by the time they reached the Astoria in London, the single had peaked at No. 8. It remained in the *Gallup* Top 75 for eight weeks and sold over 150,000 copies.

Of course, this was only the beginning. In truth, Blur were still noticeably amateurish as a live band, lacking any great rapport with their audience and failing to satisfy the conflicting expectations of their diverse fans. On the one hand, they were teenybop sensations, hoping to fill the shoes of Bros or New Kids On The Block on the pin-up pages of *Smash Hits*. On the other hand, they were serious musicians, aspiring to the critical approbation of journalists on the *NME* and *Melody Maker*. As a consequence, they came across as neither one thing nor the other. The crowd came expecting indie-pop, but instead, as writer and broadcaster Stuart Maconie recalls, they got 'The Theatre of Cruelty meets the Beatles at the Star Club, Hamburg'. Blur's diverse influences came across as a bit of a dog's dinner, with moments of hard rock and psychedelia but mostly just 'Vortex 1976-vintage punk dotted with weird plinkety-plonk keyboard asides and Graham's technically masterful guitar playing'.

Damon was already privately predicting world domination, but for the time being he remained publicly restrained. 'I think people have just got to give us a chance to put out an album, or a couple of albums, before they start forming opinions,' he told *Siren* magazine. 'There's a lot more to come.'

However, that cool reticence soon evaporated in favour of no-holds-barred hyperbole and sheer, unadulterated cheek. The first and most notable example of this bridge-burning was at their homecoming gig at Essex University in Colchester. *Select* journalist David Cavanagh tagged along and succeeded in helping Blur to dig their own grave deeper and deeper until they became the most hated band in Essex history.

Smells like team spirit

'Places like Colchester celebrate the mediocre, y'know?' said Damon glibly, as the tour bus made its way from London up the A12 towards the south-east coast. 'I don't really have any fond memories of the place at all,' he continued, setting out his band's manifesto and trashing his home town in one fell swoop. 'See, places like Colchester stifle you. It's one of these places which isn't quite wealthy but also isn't quite poverty-stricken. There's a strong inclination for people to just get their lives out of the way. And that is at the centre of what we hate. Everything we do has a subtle jibe at that suburban way of thinking.

'I never felt like I belonged here at all. At school I was seen as horrendously arrogant. In Colchester there's an unwritten law that you can talk about it but never achieve it.'

'There's a wonderful bit in [Laurie Lee's autobiography] *Cider With Rosie*,' pointed out Alex, 'where a local guy goes off and becomes really successful. And he comes back...and they kill him.'

'See that tower-block?' said Damon as he took Cavanagh on a Black Museum-style tour of Colchester. 'Biggest heroin problem in the Southeast. There's this really famous story about how one couple went up on the roof one day when it was really sunny, and shot up on smack. And they decided to have sex while they were up there. And while they're shagging she goes into spasms and convulsions, cos of the heroin or whatever...and he can't get it out! She's holding on like this [he indicates a painful vice-like grip] and they have to get an ambulance to come and lift them down off the roof of the building — stuck together, this is — and take them to hospital, where they give her some muscle relaxants and pull him out. Ha haaaaa. Faaa-kin' hell.'

Damon: 'When I was thirteen I was walking around quite a hard comprehensive school with a violin, an earring and a Karl Marx book. Which was not normal. But now I walk around in trainers and a Chelsea top.'

Damon's final word was yet another bolshy challenge to no one in particular, mouthing off and earning an overnight reputation for providing lascivious journos with great copy. 'We're not new age hippies by any means,' he said, apropos of nothing. 'We just hate the nihilism that has existed in this country for so long. You don't get it on the continent. They've got a much healthier attitude towards being young. The English really don't like the show-offs. They love it when you fail. Well, fuck them. We're not going to.'

Unfortunately, all that big talk may have sold a few magazines and music papers, but it didn't necessarily sell records.

The next step in Blur's plan was 'Bang', another upbeat baggy number with a bleak refrain which was released as a single in July. Disappointingly it only reached No. 24, despite a much talked-about appearance on *Top Of The Pops* during which Damon pranced around like a jester with a cardboard chicken.

It's another upbeat-sounding baggy ditty, and the first Blur song to betray signs of Damon's real inspirations. You can imagine the humdrum inertia of London life swimming uncontrollably around and below him with the words: 'Waiting for an underground train to rumble underneath my feet, Bang goes another day, Where it went I could not say'. Later, his songwriting would develop into something more voyeuristic and stylized, but 'Bang' is a rather more personal look at the early days of a bedsit pop star with visions of country houses.

Their first Top 10 hit had been a surprise, but when 'Bang' didn't follow suit they were in shock. And there was worse to come. No. 24 was the highest placing they would achieve in the singles chart for nearly three years. On the eve of the release of their debut album, the music scene was slipping away from Blur inch by inch. More than that, it was slipping away from British pop music altogether. A song called 'Smells Like Teen Spirit' was about to remind the nation just who invented rock'n'roll in the first place, and start a Yankee invasion that would eventually leave Blur out in the cold and close to disaster.

"I used to destroy things when I was a kid. I had a **bionic** man and **I used** to **slam** his **arms** off in **windows.** I have *such* guilt about that, because I love toys so much. I feel guilt, terrifically, more than anything else."

Graham

Damon: 'I don't mind kissing men at all... I don't wank over men. If you think about men when you're on your own and you want to have a wank, then you've got an interest in men which is homosexual'.

Wear Me Down

When their debut album, *Leisure*, was released on August 27, 1991, Blur still seemed to have the world at their feet. Damon, as cocky as ever, claimed that it was not only a landmark for the band, but for the British music scene. Specifically, it was the album which would 'kill baggy'.

'That baggy thing was the end of that hedonistic optimism that the Thatcher years promoted to no avail,' he pronounced, haughtily. 'We're not a political band, but I think we're definitely a reaction to all of that.'

As it happened, the baggy scene had already run its course, along with most of the other proto- indie-dance trends of the day, like 'shoegazing' and the media-contrived 'scene that celebrates itself'. But Damon's big mouth once again earned him a few column inches and no doubt contributed to one or two record sales.

On the strength of 'There's No Other Way' alone, the album was bound to be a respectable success. As Alexis Petridis wrote in *Lime Lizard* magazine: 'This review is pretty irrelevant; for the time being at least, Blur are stars and if *Leisure* was pressed onto vinyl made from potentially lethal radioactive waste and rancid offal crawling with mad cow disease, it would still sell by the bucketload.'

In fact, that turned out to be a bit optimistic. *Leisure* made it to No. 7 in the *Gallup* album charts but soon disappeared, dropping off the list altogether after only six weeks. Released in America on the SBK label, home to teen hunk Vanilla Ice, *Leisure* sunk without a trace.

Likewise critically, there was scarcely a landslide in their favour, although reviews erred towards the positive and a few journos were downright adoring, like the *Melody*

Damon: 'On *Leisure*, the lyrics were deliberately non-political, completely, but that's not going to be the case for the next album. They will be apolitical, but they won't be as blank.'

Maker's Everett True: '*Leisure*, the new album from Blur, is a celebration of just that. Within its twelve BANG!-up-to-the-minute grooves you'll find a love of life and music and all the attendant thrills and spills that happen in between. *Leisure* is an album (self)obsessed with finding the next big buzz, the next big joyride, the next partner to help banish all cares...'

Looking back on it today, the album pales in comparison to Blur's later work. 'There's No Other Way' shines out as a great pop single that — nudged up the chart by a brilliant video promo featuring the band in a Mike Leigh-style suburban sitting room limbo — fully deserves a place in any record collection. However, tracks like 'She's So

High' — a hangover from their days as the shambling Seymour — sound hopelessly dated and ineffectual.

In addition to the three already-released singles, the other nine tracks were a mixed bag. Like 'She's So High', there's a laid-back, dizzying feel to 'Slow Down' and plenty of buzzing, distorted guitar fouling up the pretty pop sound. But Graham's very conventional guitar strumming is a hint at a grunge sound which does not suit them, particularly given that this should be a rather sweet love song with all the requisite Ah-aah-aahs and Ooh-oooh-ooohs.

'Repetition' (easily confused with the previous track because it repeats the words 'slow down' several times) stands out technically. Graham's inspirational riffing is some of the most infectious and distinctive on the album and Damon's loud-hailer vocals are cool and edgy. From such an ambitious, go-getting band it's a bit of an anomaly with its resolutely downbeat lyrics paraphrasing Samuel Beckett ('Try try try, All things remain the same, So why try again?'), and

Justine first spotted Damon hanging around outside the Camden Falcon: 'I thought he was the handsomest boy I'd ever seen in my life.'

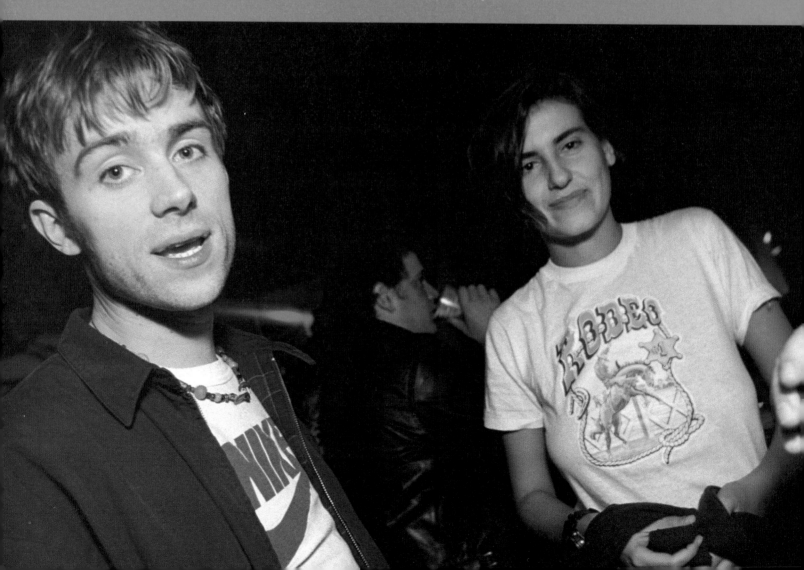

it all goes on just a little bit too long, a reflection of Damon's own feelings on a specific matter: 'I sensed that [there is no point in trying] one Christmas morning when I was nineteen being chased across my old school field by my old girlfriend's irate father. I was drunk and had wanted to tell her I loved her. There's an enormous emotional reason behind that song, but does the world give a fuck?'

'Bad Day' utilizes the classic baggy drum beat which the Stone Roses more or less made their own. It's a mix-and-match of a song, a collage of generic pop, with Damon's affected dying-on-the-vine vocals and so-uncool-it's-cool Casio keyboards. Graham's lacklustre strumming once again fails to enthuse, although there are a few off-kilter notes halfway through which indicate the unique direction his playing would later take.

Contrarily, 'Sing' is far more original, a banged-out 'Chopsticks' on Valium with a monotone vocal from the pits of depression ('So what's the worth in all of this, If the child in your head, If the child is dead'). But the most depressing thing about it is the realization that Blur just didn't have enough songs to make a whole album.

'Fool' is an indication of a band torn between commercial appeal and personal expression. On the one hand it's a pretty ordinary indie, guitar, pop, love song with a chorus of 'aaah-aaahs', but on the other hand it has moments of such abrupt tempo-change that you have to check to see if there's a scratch on the record or a big greasy fingerprint on the CD. Again, it doesn't quite succeed and the result is a bland tune with a few disconcerting jolts into the realms of the alternative.

If Blur were ever compared to the likes of shoegazers Chapterhouse, then 'Come Together' is the reason. This horrible rubbish, with its blindly self-centred sentiment and swirling, unimaginative, two-chord guitar whine is highly out-dated and annoying.

Damon: 'I used to go to loads of parties and when I got there Graham would be lying on the floor like a human doormat.'

Damon: 'Being in a band is like having a mental illness, living in an institution—you become completely obsessed and ruled by your environment. And our environment is the music press, our feelings, our friends and the audience.'

On *Leisure* you're never far away from a baggy drum/bass duet and this is no exception, but 'High Cool' does prove that Damon has some balls. Most of his early songs are very passive and hopeless, but this is a rawer, more gutsy sound set to a stark, funky guitar riff and the words are bolder and marginally more dominant. Maybe, just for once, he wrote a song when he was feeling happy and confident.

Much as the joyous occasion of the anniversary of one's birth has inspired great cheer from the likes of Altered Images and Stevie Wonder, for Damon Albarn 'Birthday' is a 'pathetic day' in which to remember life's failures. Still, there's never any excuse for self-pity, especially when it descends into drawling Seattle-ite grunge like this.

The final track is less baggy than might have been expected. Dave's drum sound on 'Wear Me Down' is from the straight-ahead in-yer-face rock school, Damon — bored of playing the foppish lover — gets as close as he's ever likely to get to rock'n'roll, and Graham even has two full-on Richie Blackmore-style guitar solos, the second of which closes the album with a dark howl of feedback trailing off to shut-down.

There are a few signposts to their developing style, such as 'Sing' which, although lacking the all important ingredients of melody and humour, hints at Graham and Damon's appetite for the avant-garde, and 'High Cool', on which Damon lets his Essex Attitude have a brief outing.

These moments aside, the album is primarily glossy indie pop with all the rough spots ironed out by producer Stephen Street, who became a legendary knob-twiddler while at the control desk for three of the Smiths' LPs and

"We're very serious emotionally. I mean we create emotions inpeople—and not just good emotions, crap emotions as well. That's our strong point: emotive music... lyrically erudite."

Damon

33

recently worked on the highly successful Cranberries albums. In retrospect, the band are inclined to dismiss their first outing, and that is probably wise.

A duty larger than life

It was obvious that Blur were going to have to work hard to maintain and improve on their initial hits. But that was okay. They were ready. 'Selling a lot of records makes you want to be a lot better,' Damon told *Siren* magazine. 'Y'know, not compromise one iota. The more successful you get, the more important it is to be yourself because you're opening yourself up to so many more people. If you go down an avenue which isn't pure and reasoned, then you just get completely fucked up. I've seen people who've started to sell a lot of records and the music's just become less important, it's just part of the machine.'

He had finally got a taste of the fame he had always wanted and, so he claims, had always been his destiny. He began to realize how much his life had changed one day when his mum put on an art show launch in Sudbury and the the place was full of girls who had come to meet him and get his autograph. He was damned if he was going to give that up now and he took on his fame like a yoke of responsibility. As a pop star, he felt his duty was to be larger than life. 'You're representing youth in front of this incredible audience of ten million people,' he said, using *Top Of The Pops* as an illustration of his career peak so far. 'It's your duty to…put the knife in. That's the point when you should really start to become incredibly great. There can be no modesty. I don't believe in modesty when you're playing in front of ten million people. I believe in just…blossoming into something great, something legendary.'

There's no doubt that Damon's already massive ego had been given a big boost by his Top 10 single and LP, and this strange logic was his way of justifying his big-headed Pop Star personality.

'If I felt I could do more for the world by giving this up and travelling around England with a guitar and just singing, I'd do it,' he said, seriously. 'If I was in Central Africa, that would be a more worthwhile thing to do, but

Dave: 'Oh dear, I think we're going to claim we've invented everything again.'

we live in such a complex society that my role as someone who entertains and lifts spirits only works on a level that is satisfied by me becoming incredibly famous and successful. The familiarity to people of what we do is important… It's important to me, because I feel I've got the ability to lift people's spirits and give them something.'

Of course, by this argument, what he gives his audience is nothing more than fair exchange for the awe that they bestow on him. 'When I sing certain songs,' he continues, 'and I can see people singing along and they're lyrics which mean something to me — the fact that they know the words is rewarding. That's an absolute, the communication with people. I like working towards certain absolutes…striving for a state of being which doesn't allow unnecessary arrogance and selfishness. I can't see the point in getting up in the morning if you're not going to better yourself. I mean, I know we're not perceived as the coolest of bands...but six months ago no one would've been interested in coming to our gigs and now we're...growing in stature in people's heads, purely because we're sticking to what we were. Maybe our attitudes were a little ambitious six months ago but they're more in context now.'

The things you say

In those early days, Damon even pigeonholed himself alongside pop's moral crusaders by suggesting that Blur had a role in developing impressionable teenage minds. Who can guess what the hell he was he thinking about when he said: 'I don't want to create a cerebral minefield in people's heads, like Morrissey did or Robert Smith. They used very easy references for teenagers. It's very easy to tell a teenager who's going through a chemical change that "It's not worth it, oh dear, oh dear." It's a lot harder to get through to people that they're great, that they should be totally into everything. I don't want to turn them into capitalists or selfish gits...but I know from my own background it doesn't do anyone any harm to be told they're okay.'

Such pompous remarks can be forgiven — at least partly — because Damon was just finding his feet in a whole new world. The media was bombarding him with questions which — in his naivety — he should probably not have been answering. It's the downside to celebrity — the things you say stay with you for years and the the prying eye of the media, particularly the tabloid newspapers, is lurking around every corner.

After only a very short time in the limelight, stories of Damon and Co's party-hearty lifestyle were being blown up into full-page articles. Initially, it was a lot of fun and he

Graham: 'We used to drink so much. I'd have a bottle of wine under the chair my amp was sat on and I'd swig my way through that.'

"I don't care who I snog, girls or boys. It's not a sexual thing at all, it's more of a header."

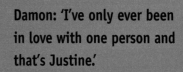

Damon

'I like things to repulse people, to upset and move them. I don't want to give people an identity, I want to give them a crisis.'

Damon: 'I've only ever been in love with one person and that's Justine.'

Justine on Damon: 'I think it's great people fancy him. I think he's lovely-looking, but that's definitely not the primary thing I find attractive about him. Those who fancy him just cos of the way he looks are probably getting the wrong end of the stick'.

even took pride in clipping their cuttings: 'The most outrageous story was "Damon was a down-and-out alcoholic drug addict who used to sing for his supper". It was "Sexy Damon of Britain's top pin-up band Blur", y'know, all the works. Better than that, though, the first thing we had in the *Daily Star* was like Blur's non-stop sex and drugs lifestyle, just two pages with photos of us…and I was coming down on the train with my girlfriend, and there was this guy in the seat opposite reading the whole thing avidly, and I was sitting there going "Oh God"…but he didn't twig at all! That was strange. Things like that are funny.

'I went to Capital Radio to do an interview,' Damon told the *Melody Maker*, 'and David Bowie was doing the same interview, but half-an-hour later. So I arrived at the Capital building in Euston and opened the car and there were ten photographers taking my picture. That's quite an unpleasant experience. And for someone like David Bowie that must happen wherever he goes.'

In a way, it was a bit of a shock to be receiving so much attention overnight and, despite himself, Damon

Damon: 'I don't think you'd have Suede without Blur. Well, I know you wouldn't.'

shied away from it a little bit. Being a control freak, he didn't like to be at the mercy of anyone, let alone an institution as powerful as a newspaper. He only liked being photographed 'when I feel it's going well and I'm in control of it,' he said, revealingly.

The shaggiest pop band

For the rest of 1991, Blur were speeding ahead on overdrive, shuttled around the world from TV appearance to gig to interview to photo shoot and back again to start from the beginning. It was a gruelling schedule, but one which left them often waiting around with nothing to do except drink themselves into oblivion.

They went from one extreme to another — playing a well-received set at the prestigious Reading Festival of alternative music and making an appearance at the *Radio One* Road Show in Skegness (where they were erroneously billed as Blue). They made a trip to the USA which, surprisingly enough, seems to have been a riotous success. 'There's No Other Way' even went into the *Billboard* Hot One 100 where it stayed for six weeks. Before they arrived, their record company made sure that they were given plenty of hype; Blur had long been described as 'the most shaggable band in pop' in the British press and that same, provocative phrase was actually used to promote the band in the USA. 'It was stickered on all our American records!' laughs Damon. 'It was taken off after the first week, though, because nobody in America knows what shaggable means!'

The reaction of the audience was almost as good as they might have expected back home. 'One of the best times was in Los Angeles when we did a lunchtime gig for K-ROQ

Damon: 'Pop people are funny in the head and the more pop they get, the funnier their heads become.'

Graham: "I'm attracted to trauma. I like things like that. I'm a born martyr."

[the hip alternative music radio station well-known for giving UK bands a leg-up in the States] at the Roxy,' said Alex on their return. 'Our initial reaction was "Oh no, this could be dodgy!" But the place was absolutely stuffed with kids bunking off school and they went absolutely fucking wild. And it was being filmed and everyone who came out into the sunlight looked completely wired and absolutely ecstatic.'

Damon seemed positively enamoured with the energy of the US music scene. 'It's different there,' he said. 'Daytime gigs, acoustic versions of songs on the radio; and generally larking about they like, as long as you're doing it

Graham: 'We can't resist being silly.'

and you're there. Over here it sometimes seems amazingly tame in comparison. It's good being here because it's a great gauge for quality. If we spent too much time over there we'd get away with being pretty shitty.'

The trip was obviously an eye-opener, revealing some of the more telling differences between British and American cultures. 'We went to Georgia…' Damon exclaimed in amazement '…and you could buy a sub-machine gun for $200 [£130] in a second-hand shop if you just had a driving licence! Which you can get when you're sixteen, so you can effectively own an Uzi when you're sixteen. Weird!'

A country where you can own an Uzi at sixteen but you can't buy a drink till you're twenty-one? For Blur, that is just downright absurd. But then again, they relish the absurd. 'Even in the most embarrassing karaoke bar on student campuses you have to have your ID,' Graham remembered. 'So a lot of kids were upset because they

'I compare us now to Wimbledon Football Club,' he told DJ Gary Crowley as 1991 came to a close. 'They rose very quickly through the divisions, you know — small pitch, not a lot of money, but they *had* something and I think that's what we've done this year. There's definitely a different set of rules now and we're competing with the big boys.'

'So, what's 1992 going to bring you?' asked Crowley.

'Warp Factor Two!' promised Graham.

'Something bigger and better, I hope,' replied Damon, more conservatively. 'Alex is going to get a serious alcohol problem, Dave already has one. We're falling like flies, Gary! We've got to be the biggest band in the world.'

As history has since proved, they were only half right. The drinking problems were guaranteed, but world fame was nothing more than a pipe dream. The international market for rock export was suddenly and overpoweringly flooded with American 'alternative' bands. The record which started it all, *Nevermind* by Nirvana, entered the UK album charts in the autumn of 1991 and didn't drop out for nearly two years. It was a scale of success that no Brit band could hope to emulate. The sound of Seattle was hip from here to Timbuktu, and grunge bands were crawling out of the underground in droves for a piece of the action: Pearl Jam, Soundgarden, Mudhoney, Nine Inch Nails, Screaming Trees, Alice In Chains...the list went on and on and on.

While Nirvanamania raged around them, Blur set off early in 1992 to tour Europe and make a visit to Japan where white, British, indie guitar bands are always guaranteed to receive a ridiculously over-the-top welcome,

couldn't get into the gigs, but we managed to do a number of early gigs — a lot of the towns have curfews, which is really weird. If you're out on the streets and under eighteen, you get fined!'

Big in Japan

They may not have been the biggest band in Britain just yet, but things were looking up. In time the paparazzi began to show up at their favourite London late-night drinking joint, the Syndrome club, on Thursday nights in Oxford Street, fuelling the band's optimism that they might be the Next Big Thing, just as David Balfe and Andy Ross had promised. In the end-of-year *Q* magazine awards they were even nominated for Best Album and Best Band, which took them completely by surprise. 'It's great, we're really crossing over everywhere,' said Damon, positively. 'We never wanted to just preach to the converted.'

often far in excess of their celebrity back home. Blur were no exception.

'The tour in Japan went really well,' says Damon. 'But — and I don't want to be horrible — all you need to get mobbed in Japan is to have blond hair and be more than five feet tall. Being mobbed is so...unrefined.'

The set each night began with a new song, 'Popscene', which would become their first and only release of 1992.

Respectability on the roller coaster

'Popscene' was a stylish combination of punk and playground which would become the template for all Blur's future hits. What's more, it was tough and arrogant where their previous efforts had been flaccid and ambivalent. Instead of letting the world pass him by and treat him like shit, Damon for once stood up and took a bite out of the music industry which he had grown to disdain.

It was recorded with producer Steve Lovell, on the advice of Food's David Balfe, and was the first time they had used real brass instruments, the backing by The Kick Horns. It's surprising that brass hadn't been used before, considering Graham's own talent as a sax player. Twisted guitar notes, grinding bass and intense drum rhythm combine with down-and-dirty horns and Damon's bilious attack on the music industry. For most fans, it was their best ever recording, but maybe it was too clever for its own good — commercially it was a disaster. It limped into the Top 75, peaked at No. 32 and vanished again after only two weeks. It was a crushing blow which revealed to the band — and their bosses at Food — just how much ground they had lost to their grungey American rivals, and Blur intentionally omitted it from their second album.

In *Smash Hits*, Sylvia Patterson described 'Popscene' as a cross between the Inspiral Carpets and the Buzzcocks, calling the result 'a bizarre commotion from hell' — a very accurate description, which is all the more ironic when you realize that she intended this as criticism rather than praise.

Immediately after this flop, they set out to regain their respectability on the Rollercoaster Tour. Described by

"The thing I really like about this band is that **every time I walk out of my door I bump into Graham,** no matter where I am! That always reassures me".

Dave

Damon as 'The English version of the Lollapalooza Tour...a real rock'n'roll circus featuring four big bands, a real value for money caravan of like-minded bands', the tour was headed up by respected Scots noise terrorists the Jesus & Mary Chain, and also featured the influential shoegazers, My Bloody Valentine (and, in a gesture towards American grunge, Dinosaur Jr.). Certainly it was a prestigious bill on which to be included, but one which most onlookers agreed did not really suit them. 'Blur's immense live energy,' wrote journalist Karen Auerbach in her review of the opening

Damon: 'I can't dance properly but I like jumping around. It's like getting electric shocks or spasms.'

"I don't think anyone who's ever counted drinking amongst their hobbies has never kissed a man".

Dave

night in Manchester, 'was sacrificed on a crowd who had just got through the doors. [Damon's] stage exuberance was only glimpsed at during the large slice of new numbers like "Never Clever" which proved that anyone who saw Blur as the lightweights of this package is severely short-sighted.' Everyone agreed that Blur had the hardest job on the tour and even the stern Pete Clark of the *Daily Mail* admitted that Blur produced 'a vivid brand of pop din', but it was largely to no avail. Their smiling, pin-up image was low on appeal for a crowd who had come prepared to be assaulted by ear drum-blistering rock. And there was worse to come.

Blue suede booze

Their next jaunt was a state-by-state forty-four-date tour of the USA. While they had enjoyed their first visit, their second was a different story altogether. With their welfare looking so bleak back home, the last place they needed to be was the USA and the constant worry about how the hell they were going to get back on track was rapidly tearing

the band apart. As Alex said later, 'There was a point on that tour when everyone had a black eye — and I had two.'

Every day in a different, yet somehow eerily similar city, they would get off the bus, sign CDs at a local store, go to a radio station and do an interview where, as Damon says, 'they'd think we were from Manchester', before finally making it to the gig. 'Actually playing onstage was the only release we got from the constant irritation,' sighs Damon. 'We just became completely exhausted.'

Of course, anyone who has ever been on such a tour of the USA — luxury coaches, limousines, everything bought and paid for before you arrive — will tell you that it is the easiest thing in the world for a band to do. It certainly beats driving two hundred miles in a Transit van up the M1, sharing the cabin with all your equipment, a couple of farting roadies and a cloud of suspicious-smelling smoke, then driving back again at two in the morning because you can't afford a hotel for the night. That's the story for a lot of hard-working, up-and-coming bands who would have little sympathy for Blur's predicament. But the situation was not quite so black and white. For a start, there was the situation back home. Their promising career was slipping away and their best efforts couldn't put it right, so they tried to escape it by drinking. Not just socially, not even just excessively, but dangerously. 'We were at rock bottom,' Alex admits. 'Our relationships with each other were awful. We were practically hospital cases.'

And on top of all that, there was another niggling symptom of alcoholic paranoia gnawing away at Damon's fevered mind. Back home, he had begun a relationship with guitarist Justine Frischmann, whose own band, Elastica, would later spearhead the new wave of new wave. Justine was an architecture graduate who had lived with Brett Anderson of Suede while they were both students at University College, London. She herself had been a member of Suede until they were signed in October 1991, and Damon had effectively been the cause of splitting both the couple and the band. As a result, a deepening rivalry had developed between Damon and Brett, with both parties firing off groundless allegations and hurtful insults via the all-too-accommodating music press. What made things worse for Damon was that Suede — despite the popularity of Nirvana *et al* — were becoming extremely popular in the UK, while Blur were losing ground at a rate of knots.

No more vacuous songs

Ironically, the rapid rise of Suede's fortunes was not unlike Blur's. They were touted by the music press before they had a single out and had been on countless magazine covers, including the top-selling *Q* magazine, long before their first album belatedly arrived in 1993. To Damon, in his deluded and panicked state, it seemed as though Brett had sneaked on to the music scene on Blur's coat-tails. 'What I objected to was their self-obsession,' Damon commented later. 'The whole thing was so tied up with predictable machismo, and it's not

easy when you see your girlfriend's ex-band start to do well. I was a bit of a prat about it, but I had to be at the time.'

Of course, once Damon and Brett got started, their whole bands were dragged into the fight. In one of the best lines from the contretemps, Alex once pithily summed up Suede with the words: 'Borrowed money. Borrowed talent. Borrowed quotes. Borrowed time... At a good rate of interest.'

Although Damon now looks back on the period as something of an embarrassment, he still feels that he did both Brett and Justine a big favour. 'They were both at architecture school living a quite idyllic, unthreatening life,' he says, not a little patronizingly, 'and I don't think there

Damon: 'I love dogs, but I couldn't eat a whole one. Ha ha.'

was any great deal of ambition, and I came in — who was genuinely psychotic about getting on — and totally kicked them both up the arse. I gave them that injection, and then when he suddenly stole a bit of what I was about, it made me go... [mimes Incredible Hulk]...grrrrggghhh, Dr Banner.'

Even so, it's one thing to slag off your girlfriend's ex-boyfriend's band in private, it's another thing altogether when your words end up splashed all over the music papers. 'It had got to the stage where every time I got drunk I got very nasty about Suede,' confesses Damon. 'I just couldn't see the wood for the trees because of Justine.

They felt slighted and they wanted revenge; I can understand they hated us with a passion. And I knew from the things they said that they were going to be big. I was just in a very bad way.'

The simple fact is that Damon was upset because his career was in trouble and he was terrified. 'All it boils down to in the end,' he now freely admits, 'is that Suede had a really good year [in 1992] and we had a really bad year.'

Fortunately, some good did come from all of this back-biting. 'It certainly fucking motivated us,' mused Damon, when his fortunes were fairer. When he returned from America full of self-pity, Justine helped him to pull himself together and convinced him that if he really wanted to prove that Blur were Britain's best band, all he had to do was write the best songs. 'She told me to make more of an effort,' he says. 'Because I'm quite a forceful character, and there was no one else saying that. She made me feel that there was more to being in a band than just writing vacuous songs.'

Off the rails

For all their optimistic predictions at the end of 1991, 1992 had been a terrible year for Blur and things would get worse before they got better. They had earned themselves a reputation as drunkards, which they themselves endorsed on their documentary video, *Starshaped*, with its scenes of debauchery, drinking and vomiting.

'We like the idea of being sensitive lager louts,' says Damon, laughing it off.

'Yeah,' agrees Alex, 'hooligans with vision.'

Well, it's lucky they can see the funny side now. Back then, they had little to be cheerful about. 'It got to the stage where we were drinking so much we could hardly

Damon: 'The most drunk I ever got was at a private view for a college art show... I woke up in a cell and, when my vision cleared, I found myself staring at a Nepalese soldier in full uniform.'

play our instruments,' Damon sighs. 'It all ended up with a terrible gig we did with Suede at the Town & Country Club [now The Forum, London], which was supposed to be like our comeback.'

As Blur's set — a benefit in aid of the homeless — commenced, Damon warned the audience that they were going to be crap, so everyone might as well go home. In the event, he was probably right. 'We were disgusting,' Graham recalls. 'It was like being in a coma. You could see everything and your mind was working, but your bloody fingers wouldn't do what they were supposed to do.'

'We were just violent psychotics who didn't give a shit,' admits a shamefaced Damon. 'But we've come through it. The day after, I was hauled over the coals in a very nice way, and told by someone that they didn't think the band could last another six months. We were all off the rails, we'd lost it.'

He says that being in a band is like being a matador. 'You go out there and if you pull it off, the glory is quite spectacular, but at the same time no one's going to feel sorry for you if you get gorged in the stomach.'

Inevitably, they had to pull themselves together and get on with being musicians again. They went back to the studio, this time with producer Andy Partridge, the legendary studio wizard and frontman of XTC. Unfortunately, it just didn't work. Graham was physically wrecked and scarcely made it into the studio at all, while the others found Partridge to be a needlessly hard task master. They recorded three songs, all of which were shelved, before Stephen Street was brought in and they started all over again. Meanwhile, they had discovered to their horror that, due to a financial mix-up that they have never adequately explained and probably didn't even understand, they had mysteriously lost all of the royalties from their first album and were now faced with the prospect of paying back their advance.

'All the money we made on *Leisure* we lost again,' Damon recalls with a note of exhaustion. 'We were really messed around.'

'Most people think that if you've had a hit single you've got a million pounds...' says Dave.

'All it really means is that you've spent a million pounds,' explains Alex.

'...so,' Dave continues, 'the more hits you have the more money you lose.'

'We literally had no money,' says Damon. 'We couldn't even pay our rent and it got to the stage where it was touch-and-go whether or not we'd go bankrupt.'

It was rock bottom. They had no money, little sympathy from their record label and virtually no support from the Seattle-crazed press. The only way to drag themselves up from the pit of obscurity was to make some truly masterful music. And that's exactly what they did.

Modern Detritus

Apart from a rousing Christmas party at Fulham's Hibernian Club where they were supported by the briefly fashionable 'riot grrls' Huggy Bear, Blur spent the remainder of 1992 and early 1993 making sure that their second album would be an explosive return to form.

Initially, it wasn't working. By the end of 1992, they had completed twelve songs which they presented to the dread David Balfe at Food Records. He calmly rejected them, claiming that he could not hear a single in any of the dozen tracks. Dejected, they went back to the studio and when they returned they brought with them 'For Tomorrow' and 'Chemical World'.

'For Tomorrow' became our first taste of the 'new' Blur, appearing as a single in April 1993. Its shimmering acoustic guitar intro and tough Essex Man vocal was a world away from the derivative Blur of 1991. Dripping with the finery of grand production, thanks to the Duke String Quartet and the choral-style backing vocals, Blur had clearly left behind their ragged indie beginnings. The lyrical theme is the same as ever — London life speeding towards the end of the century so fast that it makes you feel dizzy and it's all you can do to keep up; unless, like Damon Albarn, you choose to stand aside and sing la la las while the rest of the world is 'hanging on for dear life'.

Damon: 'Modern life is the rubbish of the past. Rubbish in the sense of a collection of debris from the past. We all live on the rubbish; it dictates our thoughts.'

Singer, songwriter, troubadour and thespian Anthony Newley was an early influence on David Bowie and his vocal inflections are echoed today in Damon's distinctive singing voice.

"If **punk** was about getting **rid of hippies** then **I'm getting.** rid of **grunge**... people should smarten **up a bit, be** a bit **more energetic"**.

Damon

Like 'Popscene', it was an incisive pop song, clever and yet relentlessly hummable, bitter and yet memorably sweet, thanks to the presence of the strings. However, like 'Popscene', it didn't cause quite the stir that they might have hoped for, possibly because — with a sleeve featuring soaring Spitfires — it was flying just a little *too* much in the face of fashion. As Keith Cameron noted in the *NME*: 'Blur's current love affair with some mythological Merrye England where Dad chainsmokes Woodbines, Mum lets the tea spoil and Junior dreams of Diana Dors and how to get out of National Service rings a little hollow. They killed baggy, and now they're after grunge, our very own slacker boys telling us to smarten up our ideas and go exercise the bulldog...'

However, while Cameron grudgingly accepted that Blur had the makings of a great pop single, the *Melody Maker*'s Cathi Unsworth was far less sympathetic to the anti-grunge cause. 'I suppose it was too much to hope that we'd finally seen the back of Blur,' she wrote. 'I mean, just try saying their name without making a noise that sounds like vomiting.' Worse still, she went on to suggest that Blur were copying their rivals Suede on a record which 'sounded like Cockney Rebel doing a David Bowie karaoke night with extra prizes for T Rex motifs'.

Tellingly, that month's issue of *Select* featured Brett Anderson on the cover and a twelve-page pro-British feature inside titled 'Who Do You Think You Are Kidding Mr Cobain?' Included in the article were profiles of Suede, Saint Etienne, Pulp, Denim, Cud and the Auteurs. Blur got nary a mention.

However, thanks to their notorious behaviour over the last couple of years, the band still had plenty of fairweather drinking buddies in the music press, many of whom genuinely wanted to see Blur revive their previous

Alex: 'America made us realize what a wonderfully quiet, undramatic place Britain is.'

Top 10 status. All they needed was a new angle, something to finally lay waste to the opinion that Blur were no more than tail-enders of the baggy and shoegazing scenes.

It started with an *NME* photo shoot on the Clacton bandstand pavilion, near Colchester, during which Damon acquired a can of spray paint and decorated the wall with his current favourite phrase: 'Modern Life Is Rubbish'. Not surprisingly, such an unashamed public display of vandalism — no matter how philosophical — got tongues wagging, not least amongst the locals. But there was more to this stunt than a spontaneous act of graffiti. In fact it was a perfectly-timed assault on the British music scene — a new look Blur, decked out in mod atire, revolutionary where once they were rebellious, scrawling the writing on the wall for others to read,

Damon: 'People say we've changed the way we look, but I was wearing a suit at Glastonbury two years ago when the whole world had gone crusty.'

With Modern Life Is Rubbish, **Blur's diverse influences became more evident, particularly the avant-garde sound of the Cardiacs.**

"It's easy to say this now, but we find this very stimulating on a cerebral, physical, and a very spiritual level. As soon as one of those disappears off the equation, it's over".

Damon

A stage decked out like the front room of a cheap TV sitcom on the 1993 Sugary Tea Tour, 1993.

mark, learn and inwardly digest. And it just so happened that these words of wisdom were also the title of their long-awaited second LP.

Modern Life Is Rubbish came along in May 1993 and — although it only got Blur to No. 15 — it indubitably laid the foundations for their startling follow-up a year later. The press swallowed Damon's regurgitated and repackaged philosophy greedily, reprinting it as one extended advertisement for a daring yet highly successful Nineties 'concept' LP. It was a diverting exercise in taking the press for a ride, but essentially *Modern Life* was not an original idea, as Damon well knew. Indeed, the concept was nothing more than a new and distinctively English twist to the Pop Art movement.

Pop Art was so named by the art critic Lawrence Alloway back in 1952, referring to a group of radical artists in London known as the Independent Group, including sculptor Eduardo Paolozzi and painter Richard Hamilton. Hamilton put on the first Pop Art exhibition in Whitechapel in 1956 calling it This Is Tomorrow. Among his own work was a piece entitled 'Just what is it that makes today's homes so different, so appealing?' which was a cut-and-pasted collage of photographs featuring a bodybuilder posing amid shiny modern household appliances.

Killing off grunge and baggy

Perhaps it is a tribute to the radical ideas of Pop Art that Blur could claim to reinvent it musically nearly half-a-century later. Pop Art is inherently self-referential, commercial and disposable, a grab-bag of advertising, pin-ups and cultural iconography transformed by bright poster colours and upbeat, cheerful presentation. Pop Art is never original — quite the contrary, it reminds us that all the great achievements in art have been made. All that is left is the slow cycle of fashion — Art Deco nostalgia one week, New Romantics the next. It's all been done before.

'There's only a certain number of whales in the sea,' says Damon, somewhat irrelevantly, 'and there are only a certain number of ways you can do things. I feel most of them have been done. I mean, why lie? Why claim that

there's anything startlingly original about it? It is the end of an era and the trouble is no one knows where to go from here, so it's either dive into the past and forget about what's to come or try and deal with all this change. What sounds more appealing to you? That's all the album is — a mix of the past and the cynical statements of today. It's an alternative reality for a few hours, that's all. That's why I like ads and TV advertising. They're so vulgar, so cynical that in a bizarre way it's comforting.'

At the same time, of course, *Modern Life* was a stark reaction against the downbeat, heroin-fuelled grunge scene which had forced Blur's music out of the charts. 'So many vacuous bands are allowing the whole sad rock myth to continue,' Damon commented, acidly. 'It's not just pathetic, it's sinister. We toured America and I was suddenly aware of the fact that we were nothing more than marketing fodder, part of the big Pop-U-Like chain. They don't want the truth, they want a marketable set of happy tunes that will sell product, and the music press are just as guilty.'

Oh yes, America had a lot to answer for. So much so, in fact, that the album was originally going to be titled *England Versus America*. 'If punk was about getting rid of hippies, then I'm getting rid of grunge,' Damon proudly boasted to the *NME* in a moment of jingoistic, reactionary enthusiasm. 'There's the same sort of feeling around today: people should smarten up a bit, be a bit more energetic. They're walking around like hippies again — they're stooped, they've got greasy hair, there's no difference. Whether they like it or not, they're listening to Black Sabbath again. It irritates me. This album doesn't just celebrate England, it's about the sinister Americanization of this country.'

So Keith Cameron was right — they had killed baggy, and now they were out to do the same for grunge. But more importantly, as a codicil, they were killing off themselves, or at least their earlier incarnation. 'We're a very analytical band... but still people think we're just a winsome pop band,' Damon pointed out. 'Our first album *Leisure* was a

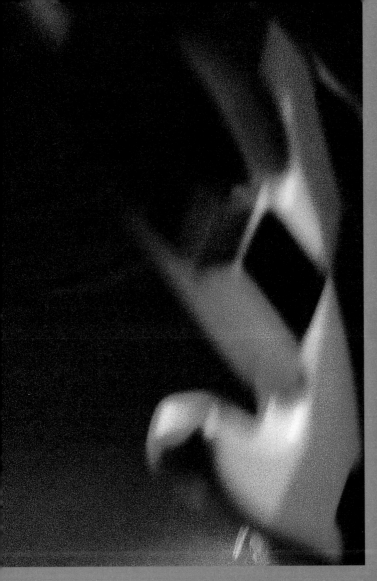

Damon: 'I haven't worked out yet whether the secret to a happy life is getting rid of your mucky habits or doing them more.'

Graham: 'We're very dissatisfied with anything that isn't slightly...twisted. I like people like John Lennon who are stars in a totally anti-star way.'

non-album; it was bland and one-dimensional and was like that on purpose. We were enjoying the whole game so we didn't care. This is our first proper record and it does have a message. Without sounding too pretentious, it's like an apocalyptic thing.'

A dream of the past

Well, it did sound too pretentious, actually, but he carried on anyway. 'Everything's falling to pieces, right?' he asked, rhetorically. 'Between me and all my friends, not one of us has any inclination to have children. Our culture has the knowledge and the right to everything, every sensation known — and we've overloaded because of it.'

'I, like just about everyone else, have this late-twentieth-ceentury obsession with the past. I dream of waking up in the past. It's a quest, a need for a simpler, less information-based way of living — a natural reaction to the speed of modern life. Nuances are transmitted so fast and information is so readily accessible that things

Graham on Modern Life: 'It was horrible trying to cram the tracks on...it could have been an eighteen-track album.'

change before people have time to understand anything about their lives at all. Ideas that once took a lifetime to think through are now encouraged into the open in a matter of weeks. Man isn't built to live at this speed. Mental illness and general angst is on the rise because people feel they no longer have control over their lives. It's a truly gruesome problem.'

And the answer to this problem? Well, there isn't one. The only way to escape the apocalypse is to stand back and watch it coming right at you. To stare it down and laugh in its face. Be an existentialist. Let the rest of the world go crazy while you watch. See the stress and strain of the modern (Americanized) world grind people into dust while you smile to yourself, knowing that, whatever happened, they would have ended up as dust sooner or later. And while you're watching it all, take a moment or two to enjoy the details — a pint of beer, a bar of chocolate, a favourite pair of jeans. 'This album is our romantic vision, our virtual world,' clarifies Damon.

'It's a metaphor for modern existence. We use pop to illustrate the death of the twentieth-century utopian vision. The music of Bolan, Bowie, the Kinks, all those represent the musical ghosts of our culture, anchor points into a time where things were better.'

The result is a deceptively light and fluffy album filled with cheery tunes and bleak lyrics, like 'Sunday Sunday' (inspired by a Yuppie consumer's ideal weekend), 'For Tomorrow' (an existential voyeur's peep into the rat race) and the particularly poignant 'Star Shaped' (about an unenlightened alcoholic going through his familiar routine of denial). Musically, it was a success on two levels — both as a pop record and as a concept. Critically it was applauded for either or both.

Bloated, blind ambition

From the very beginning it was clear that Blur's second album would be as different as promised. Lyrically, 'Advert' is an ambivalent statement, but musically it's an unambiguous volley of fire in Blur's assault on the British pop scene. Flying in the face of fashion, the cutely tinkling keyboard riff, chopping guitar, rolling bass line and ranting, angry vocal was a clear indication that Blur were not satisfied to be in the shadow of any 'scene', be it baggy or grunge.

With a tune shamelessly nicked from Julian Cope's 'Sleeping Gas' (from the classic Teardrop Explodes LP, *Kilimanjaro*), 'Colin Zeal' is the first of Damon's character songs about 'an affable man' who is outwardly confident and successful, yet beneath the bombast is just a 'retard', a twisted, empty-headed product of modern-day obsessions with health, wealth and achievement. It's an angry song,

but you have to wonder whether part of Damon's anger is directed at himself — is 'Colin Zeal' a swiping blow at the conceits of modern life or is this the writer's own way of reconciling his bloated, blind ambition with his intellectual side? Either way, this song laid down the ground rules for future hits like 'Parklife' and 'Country House'.

The unconventional rhythm, quirky tempo and modish vocals of 'Pressure On Julian' sit very comfortably

Damon: 'Silliness is an unavoidable state of being.'

Damon: 'There's only one band in British pop music who would call their album *Modern Life Is Rubbish*.'

' "Starshaped",' he said, '[is about] the shape you find yourself in when you wake up on your face, fully-clothed, after passing out drunk.'

There's a slight hint — further developed in later years — of very early David Bowie in 'Blue Jeans', a kitsch London love song set to the pastel tones of melodica and

on an album which takes Britain's musical heritage (from the Kinks to the Jam) and twists it inside out. But what is this song all about? Unquestionably it is one of Damon's most obscure lyrics and only the whispered words at the end give any indication of who Julian might be — 'Pushing trolleys in the car park from B to A then back to B. Pressure on Julian' — but who, we wonder, are the 'magical transit children' and the 'irate people with yellow tongues'? We may never know...

Unlike Blur's first LP, *Modern Life* has a sense of humour to sweeten the bitterness of its acidic tales. That musical satire pervades every track and particularly 'Starshaped', a poppy tune with Graham singing silly soprano backing vocals in counterpoint to Damon's subtle (but unmistakable) song of weekend debauchery.

piano. It's not a profound song — in fact it's a welcome reminder that sometimes life is fine just as it is, without all the intellectualizing and analysis.

As the half-way point of the album approaches, the meaning of the title *Modern Life Is Rubbish* has become pretty clear, but just in case you're in any doubt along

Damon: 'We just went into self-destruct in 1992... But when you've got absolutely nothing to lose, you sometimes come out with your best material.'

Damon: 'Graham's got that classic indie kind of quality about him. If we didn't have Graham in the band we'd probably end up being Queen or something ridiculous like that.'

comes 'Chemical World', another character song about two people living in a country not unlike our own where there is no satisfaction but ample opportunity for a quick fix. It was released as a single at the end of June 1993.

An instrumental built around a four-bar piano riff gradually and uncontrollably increasing in tempo, 'Intermission' is quirky by anyone's standards. The piano is joined first by chops of guitar, then by crashing drums and

lolling bass, as it speeds and speeds into incoherence, and the guitar degenerates into screeches of feedback, ending with one final, unanimous yet discordant crash.

The dreamworld of TV advertising is the inspiration for 'Sunday Sunday', a theme much explored in Damon's songs, but rarely so concisely and in such an extraordinarily accomplished piece. It's an epic in two-and-a-half minutes, beginning with crashing drums introducing a bouncing, ebullient tune backed by a gorgeous five-piece horn section. It's also notable as the first single (released in October 1993) in which Damon gave free rein to the influence of his friends and musical heroes, the Cardiacs — the speedy chaos of the middle eight is an hommage to his favourite band of fairground punks. As with 'Intermission', it gives Damon the chance to get his head down over the bingo organ and just go insane.

Damon is credited with the 'shopping precinct tannoy vocal' on 'Oily Water', a suitable choice of expression on an album so concerned with the culture of consumerism. Whether this is an oblique ecological comment ('I've swallowed too much oily water') or just a surreal nonesense ('It's only an early morning dream') hardly seems to matter since the driving force is not so much the song itself as Graham's reverberating guitars, echoing obstreperously throughout like machine gun bullets pummelling into a church bell. As Alex says: 'It's gratuitously nasty and My Bloody Valentine all over.'

For a commercial break

Detuned guitars, the distant slapping together of bits of wood and solemn, gentle bass back up a laconic and surreal vocal in 'Miss America'. It's another peculiar poser of a song but, as ever, the strangeness of it all is coloured with Blur's distinctive pop genius — in this case the simple 'Do do dada do' vocal hook which makes the track so hauntingly likeable, despite its erratic arrangement. For the benefit of

Damon: 'The thing you've got to understand about Blur is that there's not an ounce of rock'n'roll in us. Not any.'

65

trivia fans, the clattering and shouting at the beginning is a greeting to EMI music publisher Mike Smith, who had been out drinking with the band earlier that day. (Smith can be spotted on the back cover of *Parklife*, standing in the background between Graham and Alex.)

'Villa Rosie' starts out promising but ends up just filler. It begins with an incredible swirl of sound as Graham plays his guitar by rubbing a bottleneck against the strings, rising in pitch until it unexpectedly explodes into pounding drums and monstrous guitar chucks. But then, as suddenly, it becomes just another Blur track. After the excitement of the intro, the song seems to limp along rather slowly, a shallow tune in which Damon sings lovingly about a favourite watering hole where the losers go to drown their sorrows.

There's a Europop synth sound on 'Coping', which would later be perfected with 'Girls & Boys', and for a song with such downbeat lyrics — 'I'm too tired to care about it, Can't you see it in my face?' — it is a very speedy, upbeat, floor-filling track. It's just a shame that the tune has such an undeniable similarity to 'Colin Zeal'.

The album's biggest sell-out, the singalong, bubblegum, indie sound of 'Turn It Up' must have been a big hit with Japanese teenyboppers, who are suckers for a nice easy song with only four lines. Although it's no worse than anything on *Leisure* (if the album hadn't bombed so badly it might even have been a single), 'Turn It Up' is far too nice to belong on such a heavyweight LP. The best thing about it is the opening shriek of feedback which sounds like one of those weird electronic sound effects made by the BBC Radiophonic Workshop for *Dr Who* in the Seventies. 'When we wrote it,' says Graham, 'it seemed like a good, jangly pop song. But it turned out to be an MOR rock song.

'It's crap,' adds Damon. 'I wouldn't have had it on the album. Balfe thought it was the only song that had a vague chance of doing well in America, so he insisted on it being there... "Young & Lovely" [the B-side of "Chemical World"] should have been on the LP. But it didn't get on there and fucking "Turn It Up" did.'

The melancholy wheeze of the melodica returns on the aptly-named 'Resigned', another track with similarities to early Bowie (check out the trippy accordian-backed 'Memory Of A Free Festival' on the *Space Oddity* album), which was originally released on a free limited edition given away at the Food Christmas party in December 1991, at Brixton Academy, London. It's the longest piece on the album, clocking in at five minutes, thirteen seconds but,

NME: 'Blur have found strength through change'. On tour in 1993.

although it's a sad song, it never quite descends into self-pity. The rolling, distorted guitars almost give it the feel of a lullaby, fading away into the ether as you are rocked into oblivion by the gentle rhythm. Unfortunately, unless you switch off quickly, you'll be jerked swiftly back into reality by the album's closing fifty-six seconds.

Following in the footsteps of 'Intermission' is the closing 'Commercial Break', a lot like its predecessor only more dominated by Graham's guitar, making it far more noisy and abrupt. In a sense, the two tracks are both throwaways, just silly musical doodles bashed out by excitable kids, but the more you think back on the album as a whole, the more you realize that the these funny little instrumentals are the foundations of this exceptional Nineties concept album.

Reading light

In fashion terms, they still had a way to go. Long hair, scruffy clothes, Doc Martens for winter and Converse All Stars for summer were still very hip and there was little room for shiny Italian suits, crew cuts or parkas. The likes

Alex: 'The thing I really like about this band is that every time I walk out of my door I bump into Graham, no matter where I am! That always reassures me.'

of *Smash Hits* weren't too enamoured with the New Mod look, refusing to accept that Blur were the young soul rebels they claimed to be. '*Modern Life Is Rubbish* is about as tough as the annual I'm A Granddad Convention,' wrote Pete Stanton, dismissively, 'but it is packed with fab groovy tunes…Get it and get groovy.'

The more 'grown up' journals, on the other hand, were unfashionable enough to accept the full-package deal: philosophy, music and dress all in one. '*Modern Life Is Rubbish* is on the surface a pop dream of jaunty, tripped-out guitar pop,' wrote Cliff Jones in *Rock CD*. 'Delve deeper and the lyrics betray an unnerving urban paranoia. The combination of Bowie and Bolan references, liberal nods towards the Kinks and the Who with a Nineties feeling of loss give the album a surreal and

Graham: 'It's a very weird thing not to be able to walk to the shops without thinking of yourself as the guitarist from Blur walking to the shops.'

powerful edge... *Modern Life Is Rubbish* isn't just another album by a transient pop act, it is destined to become a vital rallying cry for the decade.'

Even so, like so many important works of art — as Damon would no doubt wish it to be known — it went largely unnoticed by the general public in its day. Initially, the album sold only about 50,000 copies. In June, 'Chemical World' was released as a single and, like 'For Tomorrow', peaked at No. 28. The follow-up, 'Sunday

people turned their backs on morbid old Matt Johnson and started heading for the tent where Blur found themselves the focal point of the festivities and, by common consent, the hit of the whole weekend.'

'That was amazing,' agrees Damon. 'It was the first time that I was ever in control of my performance. It was a lovely feeling having that whole audience singing along. And I suddenly realized what we were, I discovered the key — that sort of call-and-response reaction, that eclectic quality of gathering lots of different kinds of people together.'

Contrarily, the record sales proved that the public weren't quite ready for this eclectic pop. Blur's autumn tour of 1993 — nicknamed the Sugary Tea Tour after a line from 'Chemical World' — was a splendid return to form for several reasons. First, they had decided on a strict policy of not drinking before gigs (although drinking after gigs was more or less obligatory). Second, of course, they were openly enthusiastic about their new material. And third, they brought their album concept out on tour with them, appearing on a set decked out like a post-war bedsitting room, complete with old TV set, greasy cooker, refrigerator and standard lamp. The critics loved it: 'Blur have found strength through change,' noted the *NME*, but the audiences were less convinced. They opened each night, as they had years before in the Seymour days, with a run through of 'Intermission', a wildly avant-garde instrumental in which Damon played a childlike, repetitive melody which gradually speeded up more and more until, joined by the band, it dissolved into a melée of contradictory sounds. It was a daring debut which split the audience in half. For the pop kids in the crowd, this noise attack horribly misfired. They expected pop, but what they got, they just didn't know what to do with. Blur's hit singles got their rudimentary applause and a flurry of energetic dancing, but most of the audience left each night more confused than entertained. It seemed somehow that the philosophy had outweighed the fun. However, Damon was still full of inspiration, and in the course of the Sugary Tea Tour, he wrote the songs which would become *Parklife*.

Sunday', fared only marginally better, reaching No. 26 on its release in October.

Their appearance at the Reading Festival in August was an oasis (no pun intended — that comes much later) of truly popular approval in another difficult year. 'Blur were playing the second-stage tent on a cold Saturday night,' recalled music journo Steve Sutherland later, 'while, on the main stage, The The were boring the bollocks off the freezing crowd. Gradually, as if by some pre-arranged signal,

Girls Who Are Boys

As Blur returned to the studio to work on their third album, times were changing. The fickle British press and public had begun to grow bored of American alternative rock and looked to their own for an injection of youth and vitality. Briefly, this was provided by a few fast-riffing, post-post-punk bands like S*M*A*S*H, These Animal Men and – most notably – Elastica, whom the press grouped under the heading 'New Wave of New Wave'.

Then, in April 1994, three weeks before the release of *Parklife*, the world's music scene received a disturbing and tragic blow. Kurt Cobain, frontman of the astonishingly influential and successful Seattle grunge band, Nirvana, committed suicide in his home as a result of depression brought on by heroin addiction. The global fashion craze for grunge blew itself away overnight. When Blur's new album was released on April 25, the skies were darkening over Seattle and a new dawn was breaking over Camden Town. Britpop had arrived.

The image which Damon and the lads had been nurturing for more than twelve months suddenly and sensationally captured the imagination of the public. After two years of American alternative rock, the Top 5 was crying out for something authentically English, a reminder that Britain was capable of producing the best pop music in the world. *Parklife* revived the music scene like a dose of salts. Even the sleeve was archetypally British, a striking shot of two greyhounds on the front of a package, cunningly disguised as a trackside racing form.

The critics raved universally and ecstatically. *Parklife* was described as a 'musical feast' by *Vox* and *Select* 's editor Andrew Harrison pronounced that Blur were 'the best British band since The Smiths'. Of course, the critical

Damon: 'Pop begins in bedrooms and ends up in supermarkets.'

hyperbole was nothing new — what had changed was the attitude of the public.

Blur had touched a nerve which, quite frankly, the Smiths never could. From the opening track (and first of four singles) 'Girls & Boys', this was a sound perfectly attuned to the Nineties, a blend of kitsch irony, salt-of-the-earth sincerity and home-grown good humour, with melodies that you could hum all day long. There was no disguising the list of pop music influences, from Damon's underground heroes the Cardiacs to Britpop pioneers the Kinks and David Bowie. But this was not a derivative record, more like another concept album, a time capsule containing yet more of modern life's cultural rubbish. *Parklife* was a patchwork of recent musical history, but the chirupy Europop you might have hated in the Eighties seemed suddenly more fun when combined with a brash Mod guitar riff from the Seventies. Hey, never mind fun, it was irresistible, the kind of music that breathes life into a tedious music scene, that perks up your day when it comes on the radio and sends you rushing down to the record store with cash in hand.

The best of Blur's songs always combine irrepressible melody and sly British humour. One of the best-loved of Damon's characters, 'Tracy Jacks' is a Reggie Perrin-style hero who gives up a steady career in the civil service in order to live out his twilight years with random acts of anarchy, going 'down to Walton' and trying to throw himself into the sea and finally bulldozing 'the house he lived in, saying It's just so overrated'.

'They fascinate me, all those dead seaside towns on the East coast — Walton-on-the-Naze, Frinton,' says Damon. 'They have one guest house and it's boarded up. It's a couple of council estates, a few old houses and the bleak, bleak North Sea. They're half-places.'

Damon: 'My mum thinks I'm ultra-conservative in the way I dress. Hippy parents just don't understand why you want to wear a shirt and smart shoes.'

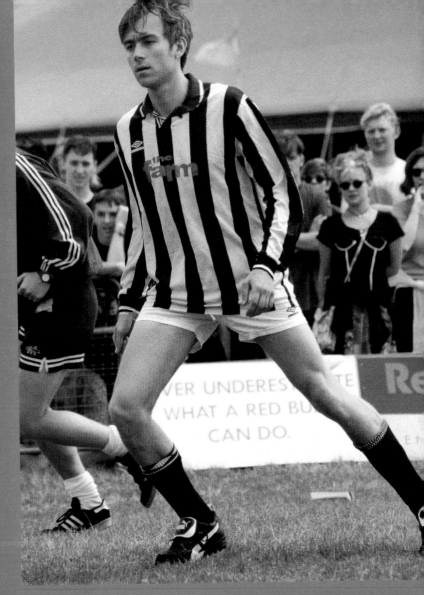

Both Britain's national game and our homegrown musical talent are on a popular high — football and Britpop haven't been this fashionable since the Sixties.

'End Of A Century' is the album's third track. With its McCartney melody and its sour-sweet trombone accompaniment and measured acoustic strumming, is too pretty to forget but too sad to have been a really big Christmas hit when it was released as a single in November.

It's no wonder that Americans find it hard to appreciate the nuances of Blur's songs, and none could be more baffling than this one. More than just another character song, 'Parklife' is a vignette of Britishness, a salt-of-the-earth, bandstand tune narrated in broad Cockney accent by actor Phil Daniels. It's a rose-tinted bit of nostalgia for a time when your front door was always left open, housewives

Going to the dogs? Far from it. Blur back on form launching *Parklife* at Walthamstow race track, 1994.

Alex: 'Sounded good on the telly...sounded shite on the night.' Live at Ally Pally.

"Ultra-normality is our bag."

Damon

gossiped over garden fences and rag-and-bone men and chimney sweeps touted their wares in the streets.

The influence of punkish mods the Jam is full on as the drums pound through a minute-and-a-half of 'Bank Holiday' — not the story of a seaside gang war, despite all its pent-up anger, but rather the ghastly ritual of the family roast dinner round the big table, which just makes going to work all the more unbearable the next day.

And then, lyrically similar to 'Resigned' (but marginally more cheerful), 'Badhead' is pretty in a way that only truly sad songs can be. Deep down, of course, the lyrics are a joke, a satirical stab at the famous English reserve. 'I'll get up around two with nothing to do,' sings Damon with feigned resignation, 'Except get a touch of flu, And I might as well grin and bear it, Because it's not worth the trouble of an argument.'

On an album which is quintessentially English there are few moments so evocative of a brass band and a 99 ice cream in Regents Park on a summer Sunday afternoon as the instrumental 'The Debt Collector'. One can only wonder at the reason for the rather depressing title — maybe for Blur there has to be a dark side to everything. Originally it was planned to include words read by Phil Daniels, but Damon couldn't think of any!

Man From Uncle-style Sixties TV sound effects introduce Alex's first Blur song, jokily titled 'Far Out', a paean to his newfound love of the sky at night, and something of a throwaway. It's not even really a finished song, hence the rather abrupt ending.

Still without a penny

Predating the Easy Listening revival by a couple of years, the atmosphere of a Parisian cabaret club complete with accordionist and sparkling mirrorball is recreated in the charming 'To The End'. Of course — as so often with Damon's lyrics — the sweet strings and lilting voice belie the truth behind the song. 'To The End' could easily be

Damon: 'Playing at Glastonbury on a lovely summer evening as the sun set was quite unbeatable, really.'

mistaken for a song about two lovers destined to be together forever, but look deeper and you realize that it's about mutual dependency: two people so exhausted by their wasted lives that they are *doomed* to be together, supporting one another as they decay and die.

Teutonic electropop programming accompanies the story of 'London Loves', another of Blur's tales of rat-race stress in which our capital city grinds down another innocent man, while Graham's scraping guitar solo — straight out of Bowie's post-Berlin, post-punk *Scary Monsters* period — twists the knife in just a little deeper. ' "London Loves" is about a character in a car driving out and fucking up, basically,' says Damon. 'I like to chart a character's story from A to B. However microscopic their environment, they do travel, and suffer some sort of psychosis on the journey.'

The stark piano intro of 'Trouble In The Message Centre' harks back to the finer moments of Orchestral Manoeuvres In The Dark, but while this track continues the synthpop theme, it is far rawer than most of *Parklife*, with a melody reminiscent of 'Advert', dominated by chugging guitar, rock'n'roll drums and gritty, bitter lyrics.

Clear guitar picking and tinkling harpsicord are the backdrop to 'Clover Over Dover', a very bleak song in which Damon asks his lover to 'roll in the clover' on the white cliffs of Dover before (and of course you can see this coming) ceremonially jumping over. Alex thought it 'came out sounding like Nirvana meets Doctor Drugs'.

Of 'Magic America' Damon's own words perhaps sum up best: 'It's not paranoid. It's just that I feel physically unwell when I'm in America. I can't help that I have this Americaphobia. I don't want us to come across as these venomous, anti-American Brits. I find it difficult to adapt to the scale of America. America eats us up. I

had to write that one seething little song and get it out of my system.'

'Jubilee' is a punk song — as only Blur could interpret the pent-up frustrations of punk — about a seventeen-year-old (born in 1977, the Queen's silver jubilee year) whose whole life seems doomed because 'he dresses incorrectly'.

Perhaps the first great song to be inspired by a shipping forecast on the radio, 'This Is A Low' is a beautiful track buoyed up by sumptuous keyboards and Graham's softly-strummed acoustic, breaking into powerful waves of sound at the end. It sets you up for the finale, which sounds not unlike 'I Do Like To Be By The Seaside' played on

Phil Daniels starred in Mike Leigh's TV play *Meantime* and Franc Roddam's *Quadrophenia*, Damon and Graham's all-time favourites.

"I don't really write about sex in our songs.

I guess it's not really a big issue in my life – I get most of my inspiration from watching adverts. Though it is a faintly sexual experience when you throw yourself into a crowd and you're getting well, fondled by 40 pairs of hands. Of both genders."

Damon

a Yamaha organ with a rhumba beat,. The closing 'Lot 105' is a quickfire instrumental in the style of 'Commercial Break'.

For the band, the warm welcome *Parklife* received was inevitably accompanied by the scrutiny of the public eye. They appeared on the front covers of countless newspapers and magazines and became unwitting pioneers of a Mod fashion revival. The phones never stopped ringing as booking agents, TV companies, journalists and even music business celebrities scrambled to get a piece of this Next Big Thing. Blur had been ready and waiting for this moment for years and they weren't about to let it slip through their fingers again. This time they were going to play to win. 'Albarn…is a quote machine,' wrote Caroline Sullivan in *The Guardian*. 'He'll make a tremendous pop celebrity.'

Nice words, but after five years they had learned not to take fairweather friends too seriously. 'They're all slumming it,' said Damon, honestly, 'and we still haven't got any bloody money.'

All that was to change as 'Girls & Boys' shot to No. 5 in the charts. Musically it was a combination of Duran Duran's Eighties synth pop and David Bowie's *Scary Monsters*-era New Wave; lyrically it was a tongue-twisting holiday snap of 18-30 clubbers having fun in the sun, without a hint of the sneering existentialist nonesense which, in hindsight, had marred Blur's last LP. In short, it was a brilliant, sing-along-if-you-think-you-can-keep-up pop tune with an intriguing, ambiguous chorus inspired by a trip to Magaluf with Justine the year before. 'The place was just equally divided between cafes serving up full English breakfast, and really tacky Essex nightclubs,' recalls Damon. 'There's a very strong sexuality about it. I just love the whole idea of it, to be honest. I love herds. All these blokes and all these girls meeting at the watering hole and

Elastica came to prominence in 1994. Their self-titled debut LP was released on Deceptive Records the folowing year.

Street doctor. He picked up the story in the *NME* when he was acting as 'guest editor' in June 1995: '[The doctor] asked me whether I had been doing any drugs. I said a bit of cocaine, dope, quite a lot of drinking, nothing very out of the ordinary. The doctor, who I thought was a bit of a prat, took my blood pressure, looked in my eyes and said that cocaine had affected my nervous system.

'The doctor slapped my wrist, gave me some anti-depressant pills and told me that it could take anything up to a year for me to feel completely normal again.

'I tried the pills for a couple of days but they did nothing for me other than make the world appear to be coming out of a transistor radio. It was no help at all, so I stopped taking them. As our workload increased, I began to feel worse and insomnia became another little demon in my head.

'I remember being on *Top Of The Pops* for the single "To The End" and thinking "I can't cope. Please, somebody switch me off." I tried a back man, a herbal man, nothing really helped and everyone had a different reason why I felt the way I did.

'To cut a few months short, I didn't go on Prozac, take heroin or anything faintly cool or rock'n'roll. I did stop taking the small amounts of cocaine that I had done before (for people with bodies like mine, it's actually a really stupid and dangerous drug to take). I stopped drinking coffee, started playing football and going down the gym twice a week. I still drink a lot and smoke a bit of dope but generally I think I've learned how to be a sane pop person.'

He summed up his near-nervous breakdown with one pithy line. 'In the Sixties, people took acid to make the world weird. Now the world is weird, people take Prozac to make it normal.'

then just...copulating. There's no morality involved. I'm not saying it should or shouldn't happen. My mind's just getting more dirty. I can't help it.'

Prozac prose

Shortly after, on the eve of their greatest ever success, Damon found himself on the verge of complete nervous exhaustion. To get away from it all, he went home to Colchester and revisited his old haunts, but rather than relaxed and mellowed he felt very disturbed by it all. As Chris Heath later wrote in *The Face*, 'When you spend all your energy racing towards the future, it's often the past that trips you up.' And so, with the ghosts of the past swimming around him, he started to get the shakes. Within a few minutes he had worked himself into a terrible panic. Scared and confused, he returned to London to see a Harley

Damon: 'I can't stand the idea of being a sad, lonely, bedsit poet. I'd much rather be preceived as loud and arrogant, because all our sensitivity's in our records.'

Damon on Parklife: 'When you get past platinum [500,000 record sales] you know it's a classic of its generation.'

Porn, cable and misfits

The next three singles didn't reach the same level of success as 'Girls & Boys', but it hardly seemed to matter because *Parklife* refused to budge from its rightful place in the album charts.

'With the release of *Parklife,* Blur have produced two unimpeachable pop masterpieces within a year,' wrote Stuart Maconie in *Select*. 'As far as guitar pop goes, [they] have become the benchmark of excellence against which everyone (and that means *everyone*) will have to be judged.'

Damon could only agree with him. 'Yes,' he boasted, 'we are the best group in Britain. And yes, I think we probably are the best British group since the Smiths. At least in our little corner of the huge arena, if not in terms of the whole curious thing. Over a period of four years, the Smiths maintained a quality and a standard that no one else could manage, and that is our aim. Plus we have the same love-hate relationship with Britain. It annoys me

when we're accused of having this nostalgic romance with a mythical lost Britain. Where are these songs about how great the country is? Nearly every one is tempered with cynicism and aggression.'

In that case, there was only one big question left to ask: if they were so damned good, how come it had taken this long for the world to take notice?

'We weren't very good when we first started,' Damon freely admitted at the time. 'It hasn't been easy to work out who we are. These two albums were recorded virtually back-to-back in the same year. We didn't consciously stop recording one and start recording the other. I suppose we just got better as time went on. There are so many variants in what we do as a band and we've now managed to consolidate all those various bits — from the quite frenetic, live, punkier side to the ballads, the comedy aspect of it, the musical side — all these things together. That combination of pop music and pantomime is, I suppose, what we're really about. It's sheer staying power that's put us in this position.

'*Modern Life* was the beginning of us having an idea of what we really wanted to do,' he continued. '*Modern Life* was us asserting our thing of wanting to be colourful and credible, a record that'd tell numerous stories instead of one. *Parklife* is the same, except it's a more radioscopic album. It's a trip through the radio bands, each song from a different station. *Modern Life* was a daytime record, full of colourful Persil adverts. *Parklife* is more nocturnal — it's porn and cable and misfits.'

By the end of the year, Blur's success had spawned a tidal wave of new Britpop wannabes, but — for the moment — no one could touch them. And if you were a West Coast grunge act expecting to come to London and

The Britpop phenomenon contributed to the revival of a few elder statesmen of the British music scene, including former Jam frontman Paul Weller.

hit the big time, you might as well have not bothered getting off the plane.

A sold-out tour culminated in an awesome appearance as headliners at the Glastonbury Festival after which the *NME*'s John Harris described them as 'Genius Avatars Of Our Pop Future. Or something'.

'It comes together wonderfully,' he oozed. 'Sunset, the last spurt of animated enjoyment before everyone crawls home, the fields rolling into the darkness while Blur plays songs as exquisite as "End Of A Century", "For Tomorrow" and an astounding, lump-throated "To The End".'

A little more than two months later, in September, they returned for a brief (and surprisingly enjoyable) tour of America with support from the up-and-coming Pulp. The nine dates (including Los Angeles, New York, Boston, Chicago, San Francisco and Toronto) were a great success, mostly selling out well in advance. Despite its distinctively

Alex: 'We've always been too friendly, too clever and too good-looking for a lot of people.'

English bent, a few discriminating Americans were able to recognize the brilliance of *Parklife*. Of course, they're not your average American kids. 'The audience that comes to see us are…' Damon struggles to find the right words, 'I mean, they come to see us on Lambrettas! They're slightly out of place as it is. I think that's what we like about them. The Blur audience in America is the most dysfunctional of all the dysfunctional tribes.'

Weird they may be, but they adore Blur with a fanaticism that would put even screaming Japanese pop girlies to shame. They thought it would never happen, but they finally got mobbed by fans in the US of A. 'In Chicago I went out of the gig and got in a taxi,' Alex enthuses, 'and the car got completely swamped. The driver couldn't move and the police came along and arrested him for obstructing the highway!'

Of course, as Damon admits, it's not like that everywhere. 'It's only in areas where the record has been big,' he explains. 'You know what it's like in America, we're big in LA but you go 50 miles down the road and we're completely meaningless. In Canada, 'Girls & Boys' was a Top 20 hit, so it's sort of a teeny thing there.'

Looking back, Damon even conceded to the *NME* that the anti-American 'sloganeering' (his word) on *Modern Life Is Rubbish* was 'a little naive', admitting that xenophobia probably wasn't the answer to Britain's problems. 'America's willingness to share its culture with everyone has resulted in everyone being American,' he postulated. 'The whole world is American. And the only reason that happened is because Americans were such a disparate bunch of people. *Everyone* is American.'

He even ended the interview with the possibility of a Transatlantic *Parklife* hanging in the air. 'Maybe one day Blur will do an American album which is all about American people and it'll go on and sell as well as *Parklife* has in

Damon: 'It's extraordinary that sixteen-year-olds thrust their breasts at me and ask me to sign them. But they do.'

Britain,' he mused. 'David Bowie did it brilliantly with *Young Americans*, and I've always thought at some point that will happen. But it can't happen till it's right, otherwise it's… Primal Scream.'

A night out with Blur

However, on his return he seemed to change his tune somewhat. In an interview with *Sun Zoom Spark* magazine he made it blatantly clear that Blur would be spending the next year or so on consolidating their hardcore audience at home and in Europe. 'I'm not going back to America till they're really gagging for it,' he said, brashly. 'I've expended enough of my energy there already. I know it's a really arrogant way of looking at it, but there's more to life than fucking yourself up. I'm in this band because I find it

Damon: 'I'm a chameleon. I find it easy to move from one mode of behaviour to another. And I don't have a problem with contradicting myself from day to day.'

immensely enjoyable and quite honestly I'm not that resilient a person to take twenty-four hours of non-stop America. It just wears me down. I don't enjoy it. If I go out there again it'll be because they really, really want me to go back. I'd much rather work hard in Europe where the food's a lot nicer and the birds are a lot prettier.

'If you want to do well in America you're best not to do well over here for a while so that the Americans think that they've found you...that they've created you. Then you can sell yourself back to this country. The Americans don't take well to a band who do really well in Britain first and have a huge critical acclaim. They're very egocentric about culture. Culture comes from America and is exported from America. They're not really looking to learn from other people — they assume that all good comes from America.'

"Of course I'm a Hedonist. What else is there to live for? The rest is just killing time".

Graham

Having said that, he was still confident that Blur would truly crack the USA one day and put Britain back on the musical map for good. 'British music has been in a backwater for the last ten years,' he said, conveniently forgetting the success of Sting and Dire Straits, to name but two. 'There's been the odd single that's had heavy rotation on MTV — bands who in the short term have done well, and then been kicked in the face by that success. The Nineties haven't spawned a proper global band, yet, and I know the connotations of thinking that way are disgusting, but if you love British pop music, then that's what's important. We've got staying power on our side.'

In the meantime, they were nominated for their first major gong — the coveted Mercury Music Prize (although the award actually went to M People) and in October they capped off a summer of success with a massive gig at the Alexandra Palace. As the fans entered the arena, each was presented with a 'Bingo Card' and before the band took to the stage there was a brief interlude for the calling of the numbers. The prize on offer was A Night Out With Blur so it should have come as no surprise to discover that every member of the audience was a winner. The show was big in every respect, from the giant, red lampshades hanging from the scaffolding to the brassy sound of the horn section in the background. It was as much of a party as a gig, which even cynical *Melody Maker* journo Andrew Mueller found

Richie Edwards (Manic Street Preachers), comedian Mark Lamarr, and Sarah Cracknell (St Etienne). Damon on Richie: 'He's a funny little fucker. The music may be abysmal, but I find him charming.'

oddly touching. He thought 'only a real bastard' could fail to applaud Blur's dramatic rise to fame and fortune and that the show was 'a triumph, one they deserved'.

Gallaghers on the rampage

The British audience had finally accepted Blur as both pop stars and eccentrics. On the Sugary Tea Tour a year earlier, a lot of punters were disappointed that they weren't seeing a pop band. After the release of *Parklife*, everyone realized that there was more to Blur than a few bouncy tunes. 'The majority of people who come to see us know what they're coming to see,' says Damon, with satisfaction. 'They know all the songs. Once you've got that, you've got such an advantage over bands who are always fighting against that unfamiliarity.'

'Here goes my big mouth again, but...' he said earlier that summer in the *NME*, 'the reason we're doing so well is because, at this particular moment in time, I don't think there's another band that have qualified what they're about in the world quite as much as we have. We've come to a point where we've really met our market full on.'

However, their unchallenged domination of the British pop scene was short-lived. In the same month that *Select* was heralding Blur as 'the best British band since The Smiths', an unknown group from the hometown of the Smiths were releasing their debut single, 'Supersonic'. Led by Noel and Liam Gallagher, Oasis were quickly gaining a reputation for electrifying gigs and drunken displays which produced plenty of fodder for the rampantly pro-British press. A series of infectious rock'n'roll singles, starting with 'Supersonic' in April, paved the way for the fastest-selling debut album of the Nineties, *Definitely Maybe*, which entered the charts at No. 1 in August. There was a new kid on the Britpop block and the competition was only just beginning to heat up.

Damon: 'I want to make music for whistling in the dark. When you're a kid and you're somewhere unfamiliar, you start whistling. That's what I'm trying to do.'

"We're voyeurs who became exhibitionists... There's a lot of teenage history which we've been voyeurs to and now which we're experiencing ourselves. Vivaciously."

Damon

The Great Escapists

1994 came to the perfect end as the boys redeemed themselves back in their home town, returning as conquering heroes by invitation from Damon and Graham's old music teacher Nigel Hildreth. Blur raised £3,000 at an utterly exclusive students-only secret Christmas gig at the Colchester Sixth Form College, a fund-raiser to send a school expedition to India to help with an orphanage project.

As the most glorious year of their lives came to a close, the band proved that they had not forgotten their roots as they got up on a stage decked out with tinsel and fairy lights to play an exclusive gig for four hundred pupils on December 16, 1994. Mr Hildreth had even arranged for the college orchestra to become Blur's backing group. The seventeen lucky students were sworn to secrecy and had to practise seven Blur songs for three weeks, including 'Tracey Jacks', 'To The End', 'End Of The Century' and 'Parklife'.

The first half of 1995 was spent locked away in the recording studio, but they did venture out once in a while to attend a few presentation ceremonies, including the Brits, where they picked up four awards, and the marginally more credible Brats, where they won the readers' award for Best Band and Best Video for 'Parklife', and the *NME* writers' award for Best Live Act and Single of the Year for 'Girls & Boys'. They even took time out to play live at a celebratory shindig at the Forum in Kentish Town, along with other award nominees, Dodgy, Echobelly and Galliano, although they were only called upon to play three numbers: 'End Of A Century', 'Jubilee' and 'To The End'. 'Three songs is nowhere near enough to satiate a gobsmacked crowd,'

Damon: 'I don't exist. Literally every day I read something that says I'm not real.'

On top of HMV and on top of the world, October 14 1995.

Damon: 'Alex writes a song every two years and they're all about planets.'

commented the *NME*'s awed Mark Sutherland, 'but their appearance still galvanizes affairs into EVENT status.'

Once the album was completed, they were committed to months of gigging, playing to massive audiences wherever they went. On Saturday June 17 they headlined at Mile End Stadium in London E3, with support from old friends the Cardiacs — whose outrageous, ridiculous, yet subtly brilliant racket was largely misunderstood, as usual. In July they warmed up for megastars R.E.M. at Milton Keynes Bowl, and in November and December they played to packed audiences in the nation's arenas, including Wembley, Sheffield, Glasgow and Manchester, among others. They also took time out to play a few smaller and more cosy venues. Perhaps the most memorable was a 'secret gig' at the Dublin Castle in Camden, which must have been the hottest place on earth at that moment. 'It was too small to do anything but play the really punky songs,' says Graham, smiling, 'and probably because it was so different from Mile End it made it so brilliant. I had a great time. We all did.'

Then, later in the year, they did a low-key tour of bizarre seaside venues, most of which had not seen a pop band on stage for decades, like the Ocean Rooms, Gorleston, near Great Yarmouth. 'It's the biggest, most happening event in Gorleston-on-Sea since the summer carnival or the last drugs bust in the town harbour,' wrote local journalist Steve Plunkett. 'Empty amusement arcades, hotels, pubs and clubs.

A desolate, dilapidated, forgotten ghost town of a seaside resort, but tonight its spirit is rekindled. Blur mania has hit town. The last time there were scenes of hysteria like this was when the Beatles played Great Yarmouth.'

The biggest event of the year — not just for Blur but for the entire Britpop music scene — was on August 14, 1995. It was the day on which Oasis were scheduled to release their long-awaited new single 'Roll With It' and, to spice up the competition between Britain's two most

talked-about bands, Blur arranged to rush-release their equally long-awaited new single on the same day. Once the word got around that the stars of Britpop were going head-to-head, the hype machines on both sides started working double overtime and before long both Blur and Oasis were gracing the front covers of national daily newspapers and music magazines alike.

Blur spared no expense with the video for their new record, which they filmed in July, hiring the controversial young artist Damien Hirst, who had recently caused a stir with his exhibit of butchered livestock pickled in formaldehyde. The artist's vision, surprisingly enough, was of 'Benny Hill on acid', a cartoonish romp starring scary actor Keith Allen (*The Yob*, *Shallow Grave*, etc) as a businessman trapped inside a giant, colourful board game something akin to *Mousetrap* — only much, much bigger. The result was a funny and very memorable promo which would undoubtedly give Blur a head start when push came to shove. 'I think because he's a respected contemporary artist it's okay to have Benny Hill girls,' joked Damon. There was nothing too *deep* about it, as Allen freely admitted. 'It's just a bloke who walks around a board in a business suit. There's no *characterization* there, darling'.

Maintaining the status quo

Like boxers psyching each other out before a big bout, the insults between the two bands began to fly, first in private, then via the newspapers and eventually between the head offices of EMI and Sony. As the big talk got stronger and more boastful, the Blur posse found it harder and harder to believe what was happening.

'I think it's a comedy rivalry,' Damon remarked.

'Everyone's asking us about it,' Alex laughed.

'Even our mums.'

'It's quite exciting, really,' admitted Damon. 'I wish I wasn't either the victim or victor of this. I'm going on holiday that week. I'm not getting involved. And I'm going to leave very specific instructions that if I come back on Sunday and we're not No. 1, someone is going to suffer some sort of grievous bodily harm.'

Controversial artist Damien Hirst directed the brilliant video for 'Country House'.

Sure, it might all be a big joke, but they were still determined to win — now more than ever before in their careers. This was the decisive moment for Blur, the chance to prove that they had the talent and the support to be top of the pops, straight to No. 1 with a bullet. 'We haven't had a No. 1,' said Damon, coldly, 'and — just to be slightly contentious for a minute — [Oasis] wouldn't be having them if we hadn't got the whole ball rolling in the first place. Because I know the environment when we put out *Modern Life Is Rubbish* and how anti- the whole idea of Britpop this country was. 'Girls & Boys' was the first real pop single that a band had put out for a long time.'

Phil Daniels: 'I don't suppose I should say anything but I reckon Oasis will be Number One cos they're more popular, aren't they? I hope it's Blur, though, cos they're my old boys.'

95

Damon: 'Thank God kids these days have got someone to look up to.'

Once again, he was taking credit for reviving the spirits of the British music scene. 'We've managed to exhume the corpse of pop music,' he said, modestly.

The mud-slinging continued right up till zero hour. Looking back, it seems that the most caustic comments came from the Mancunians while Blur's attacks were strictly satirical. An Oasis 'representative' compared Blur to Chas 'n' Dave and Alex countered by calling the Gallagher Brothers Status Quoasis.

The two singles both got their first airing on Radio One's influential *Evening Session*, and were played exclusively every night for two weeks before they were released to the rest of the networks. At first, they were both a bit of a disappointment. Blur's 'Country House' was chiruppy and cheerful, a seaside saucy postcard of a song with seemingly little long-time appeal; likewise 'Roll With It' was a disappointing Slade-style rock'n'roll singalong with easy, banal lyrics. However, when we had heard them both a thousand times and found each song intermittently rattling around our heads that long, hot summer, most Britpop fans finally concluded that these were two very fine and infectious pop singles. There wasn't much to choose between them.

Even so, the head-to-head continued. Damon appeared on the Chris Evans show on Radio One at the end of July, and when Chris played the new Oasis single Damon sang along with the words to the Quo hit 'Rocking All Over The World'. Justine Frischmann was quoted in the *NME* as calling Liam Gallagher 'thick as shit'. Responding via the *Daily Mirror*, Noel Gallagher called Blur a 'bunch of cockney wankers'.

As the day approached, the odds-on favourite to win was Oasis. With Sony's all-powerful marketing machine backing them up, the bookies agreed that the Mancunians would make Number One in week one while Blur's broader fan base would result in greater but marginally slower record sales. However, Chris Evans

"When we were finishing off the album, the National Lottery was the big thing. The advertising around it – that ghostly, godlike hand pointing at you, and that assumption of immediate happiness... You can't help alluding to the things that are around at the time you're writing. Otherwise, you're not doing your job."

Damon

97

rather gave the game away on the Wednesday preceding the Big Day when he announced the result of the mid-week chart (a closely-guarded, unpublished listing prepared for record companies but usually not made public). Although Oasis were, not surprisingly, outselling the Blur boys two-to-one up north, 'Country House' had been named the mid-week No. 1.

It was really starting to get interesting.

Battle of the bands

Damon and Justine never managed to get their holiday in the week of release. They had planned to go to Turkey, but at the last minute Elastica were offered a chance to appear on the Lollapalooza tour in the USA. Instead, Damon decided to accompany his father and mother on a trip to the Mauritius. However, he failed to remain cool and casual about the head-to-head battle.

'It was fine until Thursday night,' he remembers, 'then the whole world changed and I started to worry. By Friday I was starting to get really agitated, and then on Saturday I flew back. There was no feedback at Heathrow. I got a cab and the cabbie didn't know who I was, which was a result. Justine wasn't back from America till the Saturday night, so I went down to the cafe at the corner of my street and the lady there filled me in on all the press we'd been getting.'

The next day Damon went out to play football and when Food Records boss Andy Ross rolled up to the match in a state of inebriation, he knew that it must be good news. That day, the Battle of the Bands made it on to the

Sweeping the boards at the Brit Awards, February 23, 1995.

Damon: 'At least now we've done something that lives up to my big mouth.'

main TV news bulletins. It was a straight fight between northern, working class rockers and arty, southern, middle class pop stars, the biggest news in British music since the Stones knocked the Beatles from the No. 1 spot. The big difference was that, while the Beatles and the Stones timed their releases to share the limelight and were privately close friends, Blur and Oasis clearly seemed to loathe one-another. And the papers loved it. In the event, Blur won the day by a comfortable distance, outselling Oasis 270,000 copies to 220,000. To celebrate, the staff of Parlophone Records presented the band with a framed copy of the Gallup Top 10 run-down. Underneath the cutting was

"We've **always** seen **ourselves** as putting on **white coats** and **going** into the **lab**".

Damon on recording studios

99

Alex: 'We're contemptible show-offs. We change with the wind. We're good-looking and we say we are. We're clever and we say we are. We're not clever and we say we are. Graham's a lunatic, Damon's a cunt and I'm mad. And Dave's just a bore.'

written a quotation by Liam Gallagher: 'Better than Blur any fucking day of the week'; and beneath that was a message from Parlophone: 'Not today sunshine!'.

In truth, they were both winners — the sale of their two singles alone accounted for forty percent of all record sales in Britain during that crucial week, far more than the newly-released singles from American stars like Michael Jackson and Madonna. *The Daily Mail* reported Blur's No. 1 as 'The Pop Victory That Makes It Hip To Be Middle Class':

'The most interesting thing about all the press that surrounded the single was that it revealed this open sore in society,' Damon shudders, 'our fascination with the divide between working class and middle class people.'

Looking back, he maintains that Blur never provoked the war of words with his Mancunian rivals. 'It was all on their side,' he says. 'The irony is, if we hadn't had the thing going with Oasis, it wouldn't have been news. Everyone would have said, 'Of course they're gonna

If this is Thursday, it must be MTV. Yet another awards ceremony, November 23, 1995.

have a No. 1'. But the Oasis thing made it into something very different and, yes, I did move our release date to match theirs!'

Blur escape

Damon admits that he was the mastermind behind what became an unprecedented media circus. 'If you really want to know, the main reason was that, when Oasis got to No. 1 with 'Some Might Say', I went to their celebration party, y'know, just to say "Well done." And Liam came over and,

101

Saturday June 17 1995, Mile End Stadium, Burdett Road, London E3.

"I **wanted** them to **conquer** the **globe.** There's **more** to **life** than **just** getting **NME** and **Select** covers."

David Balfe

y'know, like he is, he goes "Number fookin' One!" right in my face. So I thought, "Okay, we'll see..." '

And, after all the name-calling, Damon was still happy to slag-off his opposite numbers in the *NME*: 'People who like Oasis who know about pop culture like them because they find them hilarious,' he said, pseudo-intellectually. 'But people who don't know about pop culture, who don't know who Ray Davies or Terry Hall is — those being *my* specific landmark people — I'm not sure they do find them funny. I don't think kids who like Oasis think it's comedy.'

'I think Liam's an absolutely brilliant frontman, I really do,' he said, but was unable to resist adding the condescending qualification: 'If I was a fifteen year-old, I'd wanna be like Liam.'

Not surprisingly, he decided to quit while he was ahead and when it came to releasing the all-important new album, Blur insured that there was no conflict with their biggest rivals. Their fourth LP appeared in September and, like *Parklife* before it, shot to the No. 1 spot, achieving triple-platinum status. Originally the title was going to include the word 'life', to make up a trilogy: *Modern Life, Parklife* and... *Sex Life* was very nearly next on the list. Alex

thought of the title of *The Great Escape*, which seemed to sum up the recurring themes of many of Blur's songs, both on the new album and throughout their career.

It was recorded in the first half of 1995, working ten hours a day at Maison Rouge Studios in Fulham Broadway, London SW6, in the shadow of Chelsea's Stamford Bridge ground (Damon's team), and also at the Townhouse Studios in Shepherd's Bush. Once again recording with producer Stephen Street, it was the first time in their career that they had been successful enough to take complete editorial control without their bosses breathing down their necks. 'I was more relaxed on this album generally,' the mellowed Damon says. 'I didn't feel the anger that I've had in the past, I didn't feel that need to be a caricature of Britishness.'

102

The result?

Damon: 'It's sadder, more intelligent on every level. It's not so brash. We're not going for the cheap laughs so much. It's about the multiplicity of escape in our lives. How many avenues of escape are there? Ordinary escape.'

Alex: 'Music is an escape, isn't it? It takes you out of yourself.'

Dave: 'Basically it's a bunch of characters trying to escape in one way or another from whatever situation they find themselves in.'

Graham: 'It's quite a doom-laden album in areas. But it's like, we're serious about the humour. Serious about being funny. I don't blame them for it, but people do listen pretty straight-faced to our music when they first hear it. There's a kind of sinister-ness to it, which is meant to be funny, a lot of it.'

Ocean of opportunity

Like *Parklife* before it, *The Great Escape* is truly a Great British album, consolidating all of the influences of life in this country in the last twenty-odd years from the point-of-view of four well-brought-up maverick young men. TV shows, high street shops, tabloid scandal,

Damon and Jarvis Cocker blending in with the homeless at a charity soccer match in aid of Shelter — Mile End, September 1995.

Secret 'warm up' for the Mile End gig at Camden's Dublin Castle.

suburbia, yuppies, mood-altering drugs and office stress, it's all there and much more. The packaging presents us with both sides of life. There's a brilliant cameo of the band — heavily caked in make-up — crowded around a VDU waiting for the stock market to crash, Damon, with a phone to his ear, wearing particularly hideous braces; Graham dressed in natty waistcoat, staring nervously at the day's figures; Alex in rapt attention as Dave explains to him the finer points of the Dow Jones. And then there's the other side of life. Blue sky, blue sea and a myriad of stars promising a hope of something better, grander and more wonderful.

'We just thought it was an ambiguous image, and it was blue as well,' says Alex, who came up with the title before the cover image was picked. 'We wanted it to be blue, because that's sort of the color of escape.' But be warned — in that deep blue ocean of opportunity there is a shark cruising slowly and inexorably past on its hunt for wide-eyed innocent prey.

The Great Escape is about the various reasons why we get up every day and spend eight or nine hours building up our ulcers, hernias and stress-related heart disease. We tell ourselves we do it because it is a means to an end, but most of the time we are too tired to enjoy that end — if it ever even comes — or (like the endless catalogue of spend-spend-spending lottery winners) we don't enjoy it when we get it. As the saying goes, you better be careful what you wish for...

From the work side comes 'Topman', 'Country House' and 'Charmless Man', tales of wideboys and bigwigs whose lives are spent on keeping up a painful and unreal exterior while inside they grow more and more crass, shallow and ignorant. And there's 'Yuko And Hiro', 'Best Days' and 'Fade Away', character studies of hard-working people who are growing to realize that a life of respectability has never brought them the rewards they once dreamed of.

On the other hand, from the side of escape come 'Mr Robinson's Quango' and 'Stereotypes', thumbnails of outwardly respectable citizens who get their kicks from a bit of kinky sex, as compared to more pathetic forms of escape like 'The Universal' and 'Ernold Same', which are about people who let their lives slip into patterns of easy monotony in order to protect themselves from the real challenges in life.

Sent to Coventry...and Milton Keynes

The album kicks off with a superbly catchy slice of Blur pop in 'Stereotypes' Its subjects are a couple of suburban swingers who escape from their humdrum responsibilities with a little bit of kinky sex. And good luck to them.

**No burgers, please, we're veggies.
Dave: 'We don't eat anything with eyes,
except potatoes.'**

Melody Maker's Paul Lester reckoned it was the most explosive LP opener since 'Smells Like Teen Spirit' kickstarted *Nevermind*.

A landmark in Blur's career, 'Country House' was written and recorded to be a hit single. Charm and affability roll off it — the obligatory singalong chorus is as banal and inoffensive as 'Didn't we have a luvverly time, the day we went to Bangor...' But from Blur, nothing is quite what it appears, and beyond the Chas'n'Dave chumminess of it all you can almost hear Damon's sly wink and wicked grin. Is it a stab at former Food owner Dave Balfe, a satire of fogey rockers like Sting, or a self-deprecating jibe at himself? Whatever, you can't stop yourself from tapping your feet and singing: 'He lives in a house, a very big house...'

Some of Blur's songs are depressing, but when they really touch a nerve they can be beautifully, wonderfully sad. 'Best Days' is one of those, a simple, rocking melody picked out on acoustic guitar with Damon's vocals effortlessly leaving

Damon: 'I kind of blank out once I'm onstage and I really don't notice getting hurt until afterwards. I mean, it's not as if I do much exercise, but I seem to have acquired a kind of stage fitness.'

Ken Livingstone MP provided the voice-over for 'Ernold Same'. Alex: 'Doesn't it make you want to commit suicide?'

you damp-eyed and reaching for the phone to call that special person who you know is home alone just like you.

A companion piece to 'Country House', 'Charmless Man' is another character song about a modern-day spiv, partying all night (chemically assisted, of course) and networking all day. With a chorus of 'na na nas' he makes his way around Soho's most exclusive wine bars, gets all the best tables at restaurants and promises the world on a platter to everyone he meets. Is he in the music business? What do *you* think?

Paired with 'Ernold Same' on the album's lyric sheet, 'Fade Away' is the definitive song of suburban purgatory. It's set to trudging, repetitive music, a waltz-like melody complete with Two-Tone horns which recall the finer moments of the Specials and Madness. It's the story of a couple who have lived their lives devoid of all spontaneity, making all the sensible choices like getting married, moving to a housing estate and working hard, but finally realizing that all their efforts have failed to make them happy. The conclusion is a bitter-sweet one — it's not too late for them to learn to enjoy life, but only if they go their separate ways. Alex said: 'That song is about Coventry and Milton Keynes and people with no souls leading empty lives, sort of happily. It needed that sort of "Ghost Town" Specials sort of feel — that sort of scary, sinister sort of feeling.'

'Topman' is a portrait of a well-dressed lager lout, one of life's chancers who learned nothing from the Eighties. It's a very light-hearted arrangement: the deep baritone 'bom bom' backup and the little fills of Arabian ambience recalling the happy-go-lucky hits of those other cheeky London chappies, Madness and Fun Boy Three.

The lavish production of 'The Universal' is perhaps the best on any Blur single to date. Although Damon's

longing voice is high in the mix, it is carried on waves of swelling strings, stirring horns and soulful backing vocals. The song itself started life during the *Parklife* sessions as a reggae calypso, but Graham thought it 'sounded like a Lilt advert' and so it was shelved. Both Alex and Food's Andy Ross lobbied for its revival and when it returned, Damon rewrote it completely. What was once a post-apocalyptic ballad set in the twenty-first century — in which the citizens of the future are being kept happy with a drug called The Universal — became instead an ominous hymn about a numb and inane Prozac Nation.

Damon: 'I like the idea of it as a Christmas single because it's not at all uplifting. It is probably a more realistic option for Christmas.'

It should be you

Damon's first ever openly political song (first heard at Alexandra Palace), 'Mr Robinson's Quango' is a slice of *Spitting Image* satire about a powerful and charming Whitehall gent who lives a comfortable life at the expense of the taxpayer and has nothing to do all day except chase his secretary around his desk and — in moments of true perviness — scrawl graffiti on toilet walls.

Once again Damon uses his early-Bowie/Anthony Newley tragic Cockney minstrel voice for 'He Thought Of Cars'. The eerie Western twang of guitar and keyboard-squelch supports a surreal sigh of a song, a daydream of escape which this time seems hopelessly out of reach. David Cavanagh writing in *MOJO* thought it very special: 'an anguished and disturbed epic of panic on the planet.'

You could be forgiven for listening to 'It Could Be You' and thinking that Damon Albarn is a condescending

Damon with James and William Street, sons of producer Stephen Street, 1995.

"We say nothing.
Dave just says nothing. Alex says nothing in an Alex way. Graham says nothing in a very negative way.
I say nothing in a roundabout way."

Damon

and arrogant git. On the one hand he stabs at our Department of National Heritage and those at Camelot who are raking in millions each week at the public's expense. On the other hand, he makes light of our dreams of buying big houses and sunning ourselves in foreign climes. It seems somehow curmudgeonly for someone so well-travelled and well-healed to make our hopes of something better sound banal. For someone who so rarely takes a stance on a controversial issue, perhaps he would have done better to keep his opinion to himself.

Blur's seaside tour, 1995.

The title comes from the National Lottery slogan, and the opening words — 'Churchill got his lucky number' — are a jab the family of Winston Churchill, who exchanged some of the wartime Prime Minister's papers for a healthy chunk of Lottery cash. The band toyed with putting a scratch card on the first 10,000 copies of the album. 'I think we're at the stage now where we could put a gratuitous gimmick on the front of an album,' joked Damon.

For a laugh, Graham taught himself the banjo as an antidote to the conventional rock sound of the guitar. The first result of his efforts is 'Ernold Same', featuring a vocal performance by Ken Livingstone, MP for Brent East, as a character who goes through the same routine again and again every day of his life, trapped in a loop of commuting back and forth forever. Still, there's a strange satisfaction to it all. Maybe for Ernold (who shares none of the quirks of his almost-namesake 'Arnold Layne' from Pink Floyd's Syd Barrett days) there's a pleasant security in knowing that tomorrow will be just like today, and yesterday, and the day before that.

Alex: "There's a little bit of that in all of us. We all do the same things and ask the same questions and answer the same questions every day, don't we?"

Da(mo)n's less savoury habits

If you thought that the star of 'Topman' was a wanker then he seems a veritable sweetheart compared to the guy in 'Globe Alone', who lives his life in constant pursuit of the glossy magazine lifestyle. He bought his car 'because he saw it on a commercial break' and a mobile phone because it 'gives him the bone'. But in truth all he's doing is turning into a demographic statistic, a lonely person with a wall of expensive 'fast-moving consumer durables' around him. The punky pace fits a life in the fast lane, although such a one-dimensional character would never appreciate its high cool of weirdness, particularly the off-kilter keyboard part in the middle, which again owes much to the influence of Damon's faves, the Cardiacs.

Damon and Justine's London home (black door). Justine says it looks 'like a bomb's hit it. We've got ten million books, twenty million records, two cats. The place is covered in cat hair, candlewax and ants.'

Alex: 'There's no mystery about why we've got much better. We work hard. Very few bands work as hard as we do. And if you work very hard you will get better.'

He may be pretty scathing about the Man of the Nineties, but at least Damon Albarn is prepared to admit that he is one of them. He is 'Dan Abnormal (The Meanie Leanie)', singing as usual in the third-person but owning up to his real identity at the end, and he's a product of the modern world. He may be wasting his life down the pub every night, out on the street at half-past eleven looking for trouble, but try to find it in your heart to forgive him, asks Damon — 'It's not his fault, We made him this way'.

'That's a name Justine gave me. I thought it was brilliant. He represents a lot of my less savoury habits. I mean, I think the song "Dan Abnormal" is about the fact that I spent quite a lot of time just getting drunk at night, going out and just doing what single people do... no, that's too bloody ambiguous, innit? What I mean to say was, I got into being completely alone. Y'know, I would find myself in Soho at three in the morning, really

At the Mile End gig, Damon said 'Country House' was about 'neurotic pop stars', but he now claims it is 'just a way of laughing at the possible scenarios of me going bananas'.

drunk and just getting into a taxi and going home to watch a dirty film or something. I mean, I've seen Justine for three weeks this year.'

Singing 'Entertain Me', Damon sounds a lot like Mark E. Smith of the Fall and it's hard to imagine he wasn't thinking of 'Hit The North' when singing the line: 'They are waiting, I hear them up in the north, and down in the south'. But in meaning it's similar to Nirvana's 'Smells Like Teen Spirit', a state of panic brought on by a feeling of inadequacy and 'guesstimates' of other people's expectations. However, Damon promises that his experience of pop stardom won't send him down the same route as Kurt Cobain: 'My pop person has actually made me feel more normal. I was uncomfortable with *not* being famous.'

Originally titled 'Japanese Workers', 'Yuko & Hiro' is a ballad about fictional characters, but the inspiration is clearly a personal one. In 1995, Damon was often heard to say that he had only seen his girlfriend Justine for three weeks and you can hear every bit of that frustration and loneliness as he sings this sad, autobiographical, love song.

The two lovers are always at work, pining and complaining in one breath: 'We're never together. I'll love you forever'. In closing, it is followed by an untitled track, sort of like a slight refrain of 'Ernold Same' on accordion.

Finding the next level

There's no doubt that in its concept, *The Great Escape* is Blur's most cohesive and well-reasoned statement about the world we live in. While *Modern Life Is Rubbish* was a clever

112

expression of Pop Art ideas and *Parklife* was a landmark in Britpop that set the standard for other English bands to follow, their fourth album was a chance for Blur to spread their wings and view this country from a darker, more distant point of view. Of course, it is all set to Damon's unerringly memorable hook-lines and chart-topping singalong choruses, songs which seem cheerful but are only masking a bitter critique. With its lush arrangements and lilting vocals, 'The Universal' sounds like a sweet serenade

Damon appeared on Channel 4 TV's *The White Room* with Ray Davies of the Kinks to perform a duet of 'Waterloo Sunset' and an improvized version of 'Parklife'.

sung by a lover to his girlfriend under the light of a silvery moon, but it's not that simple. When Damon sings 'It really, really, really could 'appen', he means it not as a dream of happy times to come, but as a warning to a declining civilization staking its future on a Prozac revolution.

If there is one overpowering target for Blur's satire on the album then it must surely be the culture of self-satisfaction which has been inspired by Prozac. 'I don't know at what point generations started being analytical,' remarks Damon, 'but we started looking at our lives as opposed to living them. That's the extraordinary thing about the Nineties — we feel separate from the rest of existence. We feel as though we know everything that's gone before and we use it all and, therefore, none of us feels real. There's never, ever been such a preoccupation

"I really do feel we've got the potential to be the first band in a long time to really cross over and stay noisy, mad and slightly dangerous."

Damon

Damon and Justine on holiday in Barbados, 1995. Damon: 'We've never taken a break between albums. Two weeks off seems like a long time to us, we just want to get back to work.'

In 1995 Dave took flying lessons and bought a plane: 'It's one of those things, like buying a yacht, that's almost expected of a pop star in decline, isn't it? Like taking up round-the-world racing.'

with defining whether people are real or not. But I hope we're getting out of that a bit now. I think everyone just wants to be a bit more naive about it all, there's less self-examination going on.'

Contrarily, Alex takes a different standpoint. 'People don't look at things enough,' he says, 'especially in America. There's not enough contemplation of the horizon.' His understanding of *The Great Escape* is that it is more a comment on our Americanized society of blind consumerism: 'Everything's sort of designed to take you away from yourself, do you know what I mean? You can't have fun without going somewhere that's made for you to have fun, as we career into the future.'

In the end, this album is not about escape, but it is

in itself a means of escaping. 'Music is a transporting form of escape from the tyranny of your conscious mind,' says Alex. 'It takes you out of yourself. So music's a form of escape, but we're all fucking trying to escape from our lives all the time. You read a newspaper on the train, you're taking yourself off the train and putting yourself into the newspaper. Do you know that Karl Marx quote that goes "Religion is the opiate of the people?" I much prefer it another way. Some wag turned it round and said the opposite is true: "Opiate is the religion of the people." We're all trying to get up there all the time. We're trying to escape from whatever, and go up to the next level.'

Wake up America!

The album was still a big hit at Christmas when 'The Universal' was released as a single, reaching No. 5 in the charts. It's clever double meaning was underlined by a superb video pastiche of Stanley Kubrick's controversial *A Clockwork Orange*, with Damon as the Malcolm McDowell character in a culturally sterile future society.

However, the same success was not true in the USA. As the year began, Damon had made headlines by shouting

115

out the challenge 'Wake up America!' when accepting an award at the Brits. In the meantime, Blur had switched from SBK Records to Virgin American in the hope that a different company (with its close links to Britain) would be able to better spread the word for them in the USA. But it was not so. In October 1995, *The Great Escape* appeared on the *Billboard* album chart for one week at No. 150. It was a slap in the face, worse than not charting at all.

After Christmas they set off for North America in the hope of improving their fortunes, but it was obvious from the beginning that they were not going to be able to compete with Oasis, whose album *What's The*

Damon ligging with Elton John.
Damon: 'Pop people seem to be preoccupied with not being forgotten. They are all trying to join the immortality club.'

Story…Morning Glory was rapidly growing in popularity, and Bush, the grunge band from London who were unknown in their home country but were packing out huge stadiums in the USA. America had woken up, alright, but it wasn't quite what Damon had in mind.

'We're pretty used to achieving mediocre record sales in America,' says Damon, resignedly. 'It's something I've learned to live with.'

The omens were bad from the very first night of the tour. Damon had a gun pointed at him while he and Alex were in a cab in the Shaw section of Washington DC. 'Damon's a cheeky fucker,' Alex said later, laughing the episode off. 'I was sitting next to him in the car, and what happened was Damon was giving the beady-eye to some homies in a car next to the cab. And I know how he looks at people — he was probably asking for trouble. Actually, Damon was probably taking the piss out of the guy, so the guy got his gun out and said "Pow-pow". I don't think it

was a close-look thing, it was more of a "Don't fucking come out here you limey git or I'll shoot you"'.

Even so, it must have shaken up Damon a little, who is nervous about being in the States at the best of times. 'I go to America and sit in a diner and just sort of go cross-eyed,' he says, 'looking at it all, at how inadequate I am in this environment. How badly I've translated what I think is necessary to translate. I haven't succeeded at all.'

English boys in America

Regarding America, Alex disagrees with Damon. 'I love the touring,' he says, gleefully. 'I can't think of anything better to do, really, than see the whole world, and play my guitar and drink beer. I'm just trying to get the best pizza in each town. And talk to the prettiest girls.'

However, although he's happy just to lie back and enjoy the ride — guns and all — he is still determined, perhaps even more than Damon, to crack the USA in the end. 'We're No. 1 in Britain, No. 1 in Iceland, No. 1 in Hong Kong, No. 2 in Denmark and No. 2 in Sweden,' he told a US journalist, reeling off the list he had learned by heart. 'It goes on and on everywhere — apart from America, where we mean jack shit. The whole world wants us except for America, so America's a market we're determined to crack.'

'This album is probably more relevant to our American cousins than our previous work, which is more in the English idiom,' he explained as if to a primary school pupil. 'We're English boys. The thing that's always bugged us is that American people can sing about America and that's fine in the rest of the world, which sort of gobbles it up. It's a big deal if you come from England and you sing about England. It shouldn't have to be a big deal — it's where we come from and it's what we're best at doing.'

But if it is true that Americans like their music to be American — even if it is by Brits like Bush who just sound American — then Blur will never be able to change that. The only way to conquer the *Billboard* chart will be to sell out, to play 'rock' music for the MTV Buzz Bin/Alternative Radio audience. Alex thinks that they could do it. 'We're genre-sluts, really,' he says, happily. 'We're all good players,

'San Francisco remains an Anglophilic town and Blur seemed genuinely taken aback to play for an American audience that knows its songs so well.' (*San Francisco Examiner* review of gig at Fillmore Theater, January 1996)

and I don't see why we should have to confine ourselves into playing in one particular style. The Beatles never did. It's whatever floats the boat, really.'

He's not sure what kind of band they are, anyway. 'I haven't got a clue who my influences are,' he says. ' I think you just pick up stuff from everywhere, really. Obviously there's music you choose to listen to, but there's also music you don't necessarily choose to listen to… It's a funny thing to talk about influence, because it suggests something of the subconscious. It's a fairly

117

Damon: 'Everyone in pop music is in danger of looking like knobheads in six months' time, and I only want to look part-knobhead.'

intangible quantity. It suggests you're not in control. But I think we're happy to steal off anybody who's really good. Once something's been done well, it's a paradigm, and everything that comes after it has to live up to it or be better.'

A focused Blur

However, it's all very well for Alex to make such a statement, but he has only ever written two Blur songs, only one of which has made it on to an LP. If Blur are to be a hit with Americans, it will have to be because Damon Albarn drastically changes his approach to songwriting... and he is showing no sign of compromising his defiantly British sound.

'Blur are a bunch of middle-class wankers trying to play hard ball with a bunch of working-class heroes.' — Noel Gallagher, Oasis.

118

'You've got to be very precious about your self-image,' he says. 'It's the most important thing that you have. If you lose that you're never gonna make good music. You just have to preserve that.'

Nothing much is going to change in Damon while he continues his cosy celebrity existence, living in a peaceful London flat with his successful girlfriend, their Habitat pine kitchen and piles of intellectual books. Only a return to hardship or the patter of tiny feet will shake him out of the blockbusting pattern of the last three Blur LPs, although he promises that he will try to impose challenge on himself. He wants to record the next album in Iceland, 'I'm drawn by the north. I want to make northern songs. Whatever that is, whatever that sounds like', and — for the first time — write music which is openly about himself.

'Obviously I'm not gonna be a *Smash Hits* teen idol that much longer. That doesn't stop me making records and things. My next album is Essex landscapes in Iceland. You can't escape what you are. It doesn't mean it's all about polar ice caps and drunken Reykjavikian yuppies! It's just something I want to do, really, just see what happens... This is certainly the first time I've got any confidence to say "I am what I am"'.

Blur have changed and yet will always remain the same. From embryonic pop stars getting pissed down at the Syndrome, to hip scenestars propping up the bar of the Good Mixer in Camden, to celebrity musos sharing a drink with Jonathan Ross at Soho's Groucho Club, it's all the same. They are the lads, out on the town and enjoying the pleasures of the flesh, shouting about their fame and fortune for all to hear. But then they retreat to the studio and produce something which elevates them above the level of drunkards, trendies and celebs. Yes, things have changed. Dave has given up drinking and has earned his pilot's licence. Alex is a connoisseur of wine and an amateur astronomer. But Graham and Damon are still the same, two kids in the school music room jamming out the tunes they love to play, dreaming of superstardom and trying to outdo one-another with style and invention. No matter how much they change, they will always be friends

"I kind of blank out once I'm onstage and I really don't notice getting hurt until afterwards. I mean, it's not as if I do much exercise, but I seem to have acquired a kind of stage fitness".

Damon

and they will always want to be bigger and better than before. 'I said in 1991 that by our third album we'd be the most important band in the country,' says Damon, with alacrity. 'And I'll say now, by 1999 we will be the most important band in the world, right? And also the moon. And maybe Mars.'

Discography

BLUR – Song By Song *Album Tracks and Singles*

Leisure

Released   August 27, 1991
Highest UK Chart Position   7
In Top 75 for 6 weeks
LP: FOODLP 6
Cassette: FOODTC 6
CD: FOODCD 6

She's So High, Bang, Slow Down, Repetition, Bad Day, Sing,
There's No Other Way, Fool, Come Together, High Cool,
Birthday, Wear Me Down.

She's So High produced by Steve Lovell and Steve Power.
Fool, Birthday and Wear Me Down produced by Mike Thorne.
Sing produced by Blur.
All others produced by Stephen Street.

'She's So High'

Released   October 20, 1990
Highest UK Chart Position   48
In the Top 75 for 3 weeks

7-inch: FOOD 26
Cassette: TCFOOD 26
'She's So High' (edit), 'I Know'

12-inch: 12FOOD 26
'She's So High' (definitive), 'Sing',
'I Know' (extended)
CD: CDFOOD 26

'She's So High' (edit), 'I Know' (extended), 'Down'; She's So
High' and 'I Know' produced by Steve Lovell and Steve
Power. 'Down' produced by Blur.

The video for 'She's So High' was aired on Jools Holland's ill-
fated revival of *Juke Box Jury* on the BBC, and it's surprising
how many people claim to have seen it given that the show
was axed due to poor viewing figures.

'Bang'

Released   August 3, 1991
Highest UK Chart Position   24
In the Top 75 for 4 weeks

7-inch: FOOD 31
Cassette: TCFOOD 31
'Bang', 'Luminous'

12-inch: 12FOOD 31
'Bang' (extended), 'Explain', 'Luminous', 'Uncle Love'
CD: CDFOOD 31

'There's No Other Way'

Released   April 20, 1991
Highest UK Chart Position   8
In the Top 75 for 8 weeks

7-inch: FOOD 29
Cassette: TCFOOD 29
'There's No Other Way', 'Inertia'

12-inch: 12FOOD 29
'There's No Other Way' (extended), 'Inertia', 'Mr Briggs',
'I'm All Over'

Remix 12-inch: 12FOODX 29
'There's No Other Way' (The Blur Remix), 'Won't Do It',
'Day Upon Day' (live)

CD: CDFOOD 29
'There's No Other Way' produced by Stephen Street. 'Inertia',
'Mr Briggs', 'I'm All Over' produced by Blur.

Damon: 'It's got a hook that will grind itself into people's
heads and then they'll come to see us and be utterly confused
that they've heard this great pop song and been suddenly
confronted by this horrendous sort of... [he trails off,
momentarily speechless] That's what motivates me. Getting
into people's homes, freaking them out. It's brilliant, y'know?
We just can't *believe* how easy it is to get into the charts.'

'Popscene'

Released   April 4, 1992
Highest UK Chart Position   32
In the Top 75 for 2 weeks
7-inch: FOOD 37
Cassette: TCFOOD 37
'Popscene', 'Mace'

12-inch: 12FOOD 37
'Popscene', 'I'm Fine', 'Mace', 'Garden Central'
CD: CDFOOD 37

'Popscene' produced by Steve Lovell. 'Mace' and 'Badgeman
Brown' produced by Blur.

Damon: 'I'd love "Popscene" to be a big hit. It'd be great. But
then again there's a noisy indie group on *Top Of The Pops* every
week now. All looking very satisfied with their Number 18.'
Graham: 'It was Nirvana going to Geffen that fucked
"Popscene" up.'

Modern Life Is Rubbish

Released   May 15, 1993
Highest UK Chart Position   15
In the Top 75 for 4 weeks

LP: FOODLP 9
Cassette: FOODTC 9
CD: FOODCD 9

For Tomorrow, Advert, Colin Zeal, Pressure On Julian, Star
Shaped, Blue Jeans, Chemical World, Intermission, Sunday
Sunday, Oily Water, Miss America, Villa Rosie, Coping, Turn
It Up, Resigned, Commercial Break.

'For Tomorrow'

Released   April 19, 1993
Highest UK Chart Position   28
In the Top 40 for 3 weeks

Cassette: TCFOOD 40
'For Tomorrow', 'Into Another', 'Hanging Over'

12-inch: 12FOOD 40
'For Tomorrow', 'Into Another', 'Hanging Over', 'Peach'

CD1: CDFOOD 40
'For Tomorrow' (Visit To Primrose Hill extended), 'Peach',
'Bone Bag'

CD2: CDFOODS 40
'For Tomorrow'and 'When The Cows Come Home' produced by
Stephen Street. 'Into Another', 'Hanging Over', 'Peach',
'Bone Bag' and 'Beachcoma' produced by Blur and John
Smith, engineered by John Smith.

NME (Keith Cameron): 'Sorry noisekids, but the "La-la-lalala"
chorus will be a fixture in your brains for weeks, loathe it
though you most assuredly will.'
Damon: 'Everyone, wherever they are in the world, knows
what la la la means."

'Chemical World'

Released   June 30, 1993
Highest UK Chart Position   28
In the Top 40 for 3 weeks

7-inch red vinyl: FOODS 45
'Chemical World', 'Maggie May'

12-inch: 12FOOD 45
'Chemical World', 'Es Schmecht', 'Young And Lovely', 'My Ark'

CD1: CDFOODS 45
'Chemical World', 'Never Clever' (live), 'Pressure On Julian'
(live), 'Come Together' (live)

CD2: CDFOOD 45
'Chemical World' (CD1) produced by Blur with Langer and
Winstanley. 'Chemical World' (CD2) produced by Stephen
Street. "Young And Lovely',
'Es Schmecht' and 'My Ark' produced by Blur. 'Never Clever',
'Pressure On Julian' and 'Come Together' recorded live at the
Glastonbury Festival, 1992 and mixed by John Smith at
Matrix Studio, London.

'Sunday Sunday'

Released   October 1993
Highest UK Chart Position   26

7-inch yellow vinyl: FOODS 46
'Sunday Sunday', 'Tell Me Tell Me'

12-inch: 12FOODS 46
'Sunday Sunday', 'Long Legged',
'Mixed Up'

CD1: CDFOODS 45
'Sunday Sunday', 'Dizzy', 'Fried', 'Shimmer

CD2: CDFOOD 45
'The Sunday Sunday Popular Community Song CD'
'Sunday Sunday', 'Daisy Bell', 'Let's All Go Down The Strand'.

'Daisy Bell' written by Harry Dacre. 'Let's All Go Down The
Strand' written by Harry Castling and CW Murphy. 'Sunday
Sunday' produced by Steve Lovell. 'Dizzy', 'Fried' and
'Shimmer' produced by Graeme Holdaway. 'Daisy Bell' and
'Let's All Go Down The Strand' produced by Blur.

Parklife

Released   April 25, 1994
Highest UK Chart Position   1

LP: FOODLP 10
Cassette: FOODTC 10
CD: FOODCD 10

Girls & Boys, Tracy Jacks, End Of A Century, Parklife, Bank
Holiday, Badhead, The Debt Collector, Far Out, To The End,
London Loves, Trouble In The Message Centre, Clover Over
Dover, Magic America, Jubilee, This Is A Low, Lot 105.

All tracks produced by Stephen Street, except 'To The End',
produced by Stephen Hague, John Smith and Blur. All tracks
engineered by John Smith. Additional engineering on 'To
The End' by Stephen Hague. Published by MCA Music.

'Girls & Boys'

Released   March 7, 1994
Highest UK Chart Position   5
In the Top 40 for 5 weeks.
7-inch: FOODS 47
Cassette: TCFOOD 47
' Girls & Boys', 'Magpie', 'People In Europe'

CD1: CDFOODS 47
'Girls & Boys', 'Magpie', 'Anniversary Waltz'

CD2: CDFOOD 47
'Girls & Boys', 'People In Europe', 'Peter Panic'

Import CD remix: Girls And Boys (PSB Radio Edit),
Girls And Boys (PSB
12-inch remix), Magpie, Anniversary Waltz. All tracks
produced by Stephen Street and engineered by John Smith.

'End Of A Century'
Released   November 7, 1994
Highest UK Chart Position   19

7-inch: FOODS 56
'End Of A Century', 'Rednecks'

12-inch: 12FOOD 56
'End Of A Century', 'Rednecks', 'Alex's Song'

CD: CDFOOD 56
'End Of A Century', 'Rednecks', 'Alex's Song'. 'End Of A
Century': Words by Albarn, music by
Albarn/Coxon/James/Rowntree. Produced by Stephen Street.
Engineered by John Smith. 'Rednecks': Words by Coxon,
music by Albarn/Coxon/James/Rowntree. 'Alex's Song':
Words and music by James.

Damon: 'It's about how couples get into staying in and staring
at each other. Only instead of candle light, it's the TV light.'

'Parklife'
Released   September 1994
Highest UK Chart Position   10

12-inch: 12FOOD 53
'Parklife', 'Supa Shoppa', 'To The End' (French version),
'Beard'

CD1: CDFOODS 53)
'Parklife', 'Supa Shoppa', 'Theme From An Imaginary Film'

CD2: CDFOOD 53
'Parklife' and 'Theme From An Imaginary Film' produced by
Stephen Street and engineered by John Smith. 'Supa
Shoppa' and 'Beard' produced by Blur and John Smith. 'To
The End' (French version) produced by Stephen Hague, John
Smith and Blur, engineered by John Smith.

'To The End'
Released   May 30, 1994
Highest UK Chart Position   16
In the Top 40 for 3 weeks

Cassette: TCFOOD 50
'To The End', 'Girls & Boys' (Pet Shop Boys 7-inch remix),
'Threadneedle Street'

12-inch: 12FOOD 50
'To The End', 'Girls & Boys" (Pet Shop Boys 7-inch remix),
'Girls & Boys (Pet Shop Boys 12-inch remix)

CD1: CDFOODS 50
'To The End', 'Threadneedle Street', 'Got Yer!'

CD2: CDFOOD 50
'To The End' produced by Stephen Hague, John Smith and
Blur. 'Girls & Boys' produced by Stephen Street, remixed by
the Pet Shop Boys. 'Threadneedle Street' and 'Got Yer!'
produced by Blur. All tracks engineered by John Smith.

The Great Escape
Released   September 11, 1995
Highest UK Chart Position   1

CD: FOODCD 14
Cassette: TCFOOD 14
LP: FOODLP 14
Stereotypes, Country House, Best Days, Charmless Man, Fade
Away, Top Man, The Universal, Mr. Robinson's Quango, He
Thought Of Cars, It Could Be You, Ernold Same, Globe Alone,
Dan Abnormal, Entertain Me, Yuko And Hiro.

'Country House'

Released	August 14, 1995
Highest UK Chart Position	1

CD1 — Blur's Country House
'Country House, 'One Born Every Minute', 'To The End' (With Francoise Hardy)
 CD2 — Blur's Country House No. 2
(Blur Recorded Live From Mile End Stadium, Saturday, June 17, 1995)
'Country House', 'Girls & Boys', 'Parklife', 'For Tomorrow'

(CD1): 'Country House' produced by Stephen Street, engineered by John Smith assisted by Tom Girling & Julia Gardner. "One Born Every Minute' produced by Blur and John Smith.
'To The End' original production by Stephen Hague, additional production by Blur; mixed by Stephen Street and John Smith; French lyrics by Francoise Hardy; Orchestra fixed by Isobel Griffiths, Conducted by Rick Wentworth; Strings arranged by Khalil Chahine; Accordion solo by Jacques Bolognesi. Francoise Hardy appears by kind permission of Virgin Records France. 'Country House' and 'One Born Every Minute' published by MCA Music Ltd.
(CD2): All tracks recorded live for Radio 1.

Damon: 'I find writing songs and catchy tunes really easy, but even with "Country House" it has to have little things in it like [rhyming] "Balzac" and "Prozac". Odd things. They're very important because, for me, that's what makes it interesting, slightly twisted pop music.'

Selected B-Sides

The story goes that 'Alex's Song' was intended to be a serious piece of music, but it ended up as another throwaway B-side on 'End Of The Century', strummed unimaginatively on guitar while he sings through a 'harmonizer' making his voice sound like a 33rpm record being played at 45.
Alex: 'They made me do it!... It's not finished. It could have been far better. Balls I say. Bollocks to them.'

Playing up to the London crowd, Blur's version of 'Daisy Bell' ('Daisy, Daisy, give me your answer do...') is performed with a not-so-traditional punk-stroke-football terrace chorus, featuring a bizarre megaphone voiceover in the bridge section. Whoever would have guessed that this song had so many lyrics? It's a novelty, for sure, but an early indication that the lads had a sense of humour. The accompanying version of 'Let's All Go Down The Strand' is comparatively straight and therefore not quite so much fun.

Fading up like the dawn into a roaring wall of sound and reckless, lo-fi percussion, 'Day Upon Day' is a relic of another era but still manages to combine jangly guitars, indie pop and art school pomp to tremendous effect. You can just imagine a fresh-faced Damon rolling on the floor of the Camden Falcon with his legs kicking in the air, totally forgetting the ten or twenty people in the so-called audience.

The crazed combination of Buzzcocks and Cardiacs conspire in Damon's mind to create the thousand mile-an-hour acid trip of 'Fried', which dates back to the days of Seymour. With all the subtlety and seriousness of 'Allo John Got A New Motor', this kind of wild, untamed brilliance was kicked into touch when Blur went into the studio to record *Leisure*. It may not have been commercial, but it was this kind of energetic, unconventional insanity which made them the band they are today.

Like something off Tom Waits's extraordinary, clattering, waltzing, brass-band bonanza, *Swordfishtrombones*, 'Got Yer' is as deep into character as Blur ever get, an hilarious and absorbing thumbnail of old man Steptoe chasing wildfowl off his property with a grumble and a twelve-bore. A perfect antidote to the sad and disturbing A-side 'To The End'.

The label says hot but the B-side says not. With a chugging guitar riff swiped from the Wonder Stuff's crowd-pleasing 'Unbearable', soaring MBV guitar on the chorus and a catchy, repetitive vocal hook, 'I'm All Over' is a prime example of the early Blur trying too hard, bursting with impressive, calculated technique but utterly lacking in imagination.
Graham: 'A ridiculous song with a terrible, synthetic drumbeat.'

For years it has been an obsession of Damon's. 'Inertia', a constant force moving in one direction without change, is a characteristic of society which frustrates him and a trend in his own personality which he despises. It's often said that true workaholics are just lazy people who overcompensate for their own idleness. The same could well be said of Blur and this soothing, half-whispered modern blues, one of many B-sides attached to 'There's No Other Way', is more personal and emotional than any track on *Leisure*.

'Here we go, Here we go again, Dirty knickers, Pop music, Vodka and gin...' How better to sum up Blur's career of philosophy, drugs and rock'n'roll. 'One Born Every Minute' is probably the best known of all their B-sides since it was the flip to their biggest-selling single, 'Country House'. It's their own 'Yellow Submarine', a nursery singalong with their usual bouncy knees-up rhythm crowded with silly duck calls and Chitty-Chitty Bang-Bang sound effects but (as always) with a hint of doom in the chorus.

The only Blur song so far to be written primarily by Graham, 'Red Necks' is hardly a masterpiece, but it is an amusing Country & Western pastiche, spoken in an authentic drunken American accent. It's about vulgar meat-heads talking bullshit at a truck stop diner ('Sure is damn good thumpage in that waitress's ass'). The original version was reputedly a thirty-minute improvized jam.

If ever proof was needed that Damon Albarn was a fan of Bertholt Brecht and Kurt Weill then 'Theme From An Imaginary Film' is it. Typical imagery
(a peasant philosopher lying in the dirt, cursing and laughing at the sun) and typical music (a potent, swirling waltz with grand synthesized strings and choir) breaking into a strident military march half-way. How wonderfully overblown and fittingly continental as a foil to 'Parklife'.

Chronology

1964

Dave Rowntree born May 8

1968

Damon Albarn born March 23

Alex James born November 1

1969

Graham Coxon born March 12

1978

The Albarn family leave their home in London to live in Colchester where Damon meets Graham at Stanway Comprehensive.

1988

Graham attends Goldsmith's College in London, where he meets Alex. Damon has already moved to London, where he does bar work and other part-time jobs, including unpaid work at recording studio The Beat Factory. Damon makes a one-off solo appearance at Colchester Arts Centre. Graham and his friend Dave are in attendance. Soon after, Damon, Graham, Alex and Dave begin recording Damon's demos together at the Beat Factory.

1989

Under the name Seymour, the four-piece play a few small gigs, mostly around the London area in small venues including Dingwalls, Camden and the Powerhaus, Islington, where they are spotted by Andy Ross of Food Records.

1990

They sign to Food in March, changing their name to Blur under pressure from the record company. Graham and Alex drop out of college to begin recording, and debut single 'She's So High' is released in October. Modest press interest pigeonholes the band as 'Baggy', and radio plays leads to a No. 48 chart placing. The year ends with an appearance at Brixton Academy supporting the Soup Dragons.

1991

Second single 'There's No Other Way' is surprise big hit, reaching No. 8 in the charts. Teen magazines, music papers and tabloid newspapers all begin to take a serious interest in Blur. *The Daily Star* is the first to unveil the truth about their debauched home life with the headline: 'Busty Girls and Long-Legged Lovelies Go Wild For Boozy Band'. However, despite intensive publicity and world touring, culminating with a showcase of Food bands at theChristmas Party back at Brixton Academy, sales of debut album *Leisure* are mildly disappointing.

1992

Reputation for drinking and partying begins to turn sour, with shambolic charity benefit at the Forum in London where supporting act Suede outshine Blur in style and attitude. With grunge fever sweeping the world, attempted comeback in March with 'Popscene' single is a damp squib. Rollercoaster Tour in April alongside My Bloody Valentine and Jesus & Mary Chain is bold attempt to gain critical respectability, but public image is marred by war of words between Damon and Suede's Brett Anderson (formerly linked – romantically and musically – to Damon's partner, Justine Frischmann). Second tour of America is source of great internal stress. On their return they are faced with financial problems and increased pressure from Food bosses anxious for a hit single.

1993

After extended absence from the scene, 'For Tomorrow' is a return to critical approbation accompanied by a new 'mod' image. Second album *Modern Life Is Rubbish* provides ample fodder for pseudo-intellectual journos, yet still American grunge dominates the hip alternative.

1994

Kitsch 'Girls & Boys' single marks a dramatic return to chart success, making Number Five in March. Follow-up album Parklife in April coincides with shock suicide of Nirvana frontman, Kurt Cobain, and a public backlash against downbeat American rock. Blur are at the spearhead of Britpop movement which celebrates the rise of homegrown talent, particularly those bands whose influences are distinctively British, for instance: The Jam, The Kinks, David Bowie. Three more singles from the album, including the definitive title track, all reach the Top 20. Respects are paid to their fans and supporters at a massive, celebratory show at Alexandra Palace in London, but the year ends stylishly with an exclusive, homecoming, students-only, fund-raising gig at Colchester Sixth Form College.

1995

While recording their fourth album they take time off to pick up major awards at the Brits and Brats. They come out of hiding to play a massive gig at Mile End stadium in June, previewing their forthcoming single 'Country House'. It is released on August 14. On the same day, the new record by their biggest rivals, Oasis, is also released. After massive hype on both sides, Blur enter the charts at No. 1, with Oasis coming a close second. The following month, *The Great Escape* enters the album chart at the top spot, achieving triple platinum sales so far, followed by the Christmas single 'The Universal' – their third Top 5 hit.

1996

'Stereotypes', lifted from the latest album, reaches No. 7 in February, closely followed by 'Charmless Man' in April, which peaks at Number 5. They are eclipsed by Oasis at the year's big awards celebrations. Although Damon claims to have 'killed Britpop', one of his solo compositions appears on the fashionable soundtrack album, *Trainspotting*, alongside Blur, Pulp, Elastica, Sleeper and other Britpop notables. He announces his intention to record the next Blur LP in Iceland, expected to be released in early 1997.

Index